Globalization and Labor

Society

opment

Rights

bor

erty

Environment

d Culture

The New Global Society

Globalization and Labor

Peter Enderwick
Auckland University of Technology, New Zealand

Foreword by
James Bacchus
Chairman, Global Trade Practice Group
of Greenberg Traurig, Professional Association

Introduction by
Ilan Alon, Ph.D.
Crummer Graduate School of Business
Rollins College

CHELSEA HOUSE
P U B L I S H E R S
A Haights Cross Communications Company ®
Philadelphia

COVER: A nine-year-old Nepali girl harvests tea on Peshok Tea Estate, Nepal

CHELSEA HOUSE PUBLISHERS

VP, NEW PRODUCT DEVELOPMENT   Sally Cheney
DIRECTOR OF PRODUCTION   Kim Shinners
CREATIVE MANAGER   Takeshi Takahashi
MANUFACTURING MANAGER   Diann Grasse

Staff for GLOBALIZATION AND LABOR

EXECUTIVE EDITOR   Lee Marcott
EDITORIAL ASSISTANT   Carla Greenberg
PRODUCTION EDITOR   Bonnie Cohen
PHOTO EDITOR   Sarah Bloom
SERIES AND COVER DESIGNER   Keith Trego
LAYOUT   21st Century Publishing and Communications, Inc.

Library of Congress Cataloging-in-Publication Data

Enderwick, Peter.
   Globalization and labor/Peter Enderwick.
      p. cm.—(The new global society)
   Includes bibliographical references and index.
   ISBN 0-7910-8187-7 (hard cover)
   1. Labor market. 2. Globalization. I. Title. II. Series.
HD5706.E55 2005
331.12'09'051—dc22

                                                2005015049

All links and web addresses were checked and verified to be correct at the time of publication. Because of the dynamic nature of the web, some addresses and links may have changed since publication and may no longer be valid.

Contents

Foreword

by James Bacchus

IT'S A SMALL WORLD AFTER ALL

One reason that I know this is true is because I have a daughter who adores Walt Disney World in my hometown of Orlando, Florida. When Jamey was small, she and I would go to Walt Disney World together. We would stand together in a long line waiting to ride her very favorite ride—"Small World." We would stand together in those long lines over and over again.

Jamey is in high school now, but, of course, she still adores Walt Disney World, and she and I still stand together from time to time in those same long lines—because she never tires of seeing "Small World." She is not alone. Seemingly endless lines of children have stood waiting for that same ride through the years, hand in hand with their parents, waiting for the chance to take the winding boat ride through Disney's "Small World." When their chance has come, they have seen the vast variety of the world in which we live unfold along the winding way as it appears to the child in all of us. Hundreds of dancing dolls adorn an array of diverse and exotic settings from around the world. In the echoing voice of a song they sing together— over and over again—they remind all those along for the ride that ours is a world of laughter, a world of tears, a world of hopes, and a world of fears.

And so it is. So it appears when we are children, and so it surely appears when we put childhood behind us and try to assume our new roles as "grown-ups" in what is supposed to be the adult world. The laughter, the tears, the hopes, the fears, are all still there in a world that, to our grown-up eyes, keeps getting smaller every day. And, even when we are no longer children, even when we are now grown-ups, we don't really know what to do about it.

The grown-up name for our small world is "globalization." Our globalizing world is getting smaller every day. Economically and otherwise, our world is becoming a place where we all seem to be taking the same ride. Advances in information, transportation, and many other technologies are making distance disappear, and are making next-door neighbors of all of us, whatever our nationality, whatever our costume, whatever the song we sing.

When Walt Disney first introduced the "Small World" ride at the World's Fair in New York in 1964, I was in high school, and we could still pretend that, although the world was getting smaller, it still consisted of many different places. But no more. The other day, I took a handheld device, called a "BlackBerry," out of my pocket and e-mailed instructions to a colleague in my law firm regarding a pending legal matter. I was on a train in the Bavarian mountains in Germany, while my colleague was thousands of miles away in the United States. In effect, we were in the same small place.

This is just one example of our ever-smaller world. And, however small it seems to me in my middle age, and however smaller it may become in my lifetime, it is likely to shrink all the more for my daughter Jamey and for every other young American attending high school today.

Hence, we announce this new series of books for high school students on some of the results of globalization. These results inspire hope, shown in the efforts of so many around the world to respond to the challenges posed by globalization by making international laws, building international institutions, and seeking new ways to live and work together in our smaller world. Those results also inspire fear, as evidenced by streets filled with anti-globalization protesters in Seattle, London, and other globalized cities around the world.

It is hard to tell truth from fiction in assessing the results of globalization. The six volumes in this series help us to do so. Does globalization promote worldwide economic development, or does it hinder it? Does it reduce poverty, or does it increase it? Does it enhance culture, or does it harm it? Does it advance the cause of human rights, or does it impede it? Does it serve the cause of workers' rights, or does it slow it? Does it help the environment, or does it hurt it? These are the important questions posed in these volumes. The hope is that in asking these questions the series will help young people find answers to them that will prove to be better than those found thus far by "grown-ups."

I have had the privilege of trying to begin the process of finding some of these answers. I have helped negotiate international trade agreements for the United States. I have served as a member of the Congress of the United States. I have been one of seven jurists worldwide on the court of final appeal that helps the 148 countries that are Members of the World Trade Organization to uphold international trade rules and to peacefully resolve international trade disputes. I am one of these who see far more reason for hope than for fear in the process of globalization.

I believe we will all be more likely to see globalization in this way if we recall the faces of the dancing dolls in Disney's "Small World." Those dolls are from many different countries. They wear many different costumes. But their faces are very much the same. The song they sing is the same. And, in that song, they remind us all that as we all ride together, "There's so much that we share, that it's time we're aware it's a small world, after all." Indeed it is. And, if we remember all that we in the world share—if we remember above all, our shared humanity—then we will be much more likely to make globalization a reason to hope that our smaller world will also be a better world.

James Bacchus
Chairman, Global Trade Practice Group
of Greenberg Traurig, Professional Association
April 2005

Introduction
by Ilan Alon

Globalization is now an omnipresent phenomenon in society, economics, and politics, affecting industry and government, and all other walks of life in one form or another. THE NEW GLOBAL SOCIETY series gives the reader a well-rounded understanding of the forces of globalization and its multifaceted impact on our world. The international flavor is evident in the make-up of the authors in the series, who include one Israeli, one New Zealander, one Bulgarian, one Korean, and two American scholars. In addition to an international slate of authors, many of whom have lived and worked around the world, the writers hail from fields as diverse as economics, business, comparative literature, and journalism. Their varied experiences and points of view bring a comprehensive and diverse analysis to the topics they write about.

While the books were written to stand alone, those readers who complete all six will find many points of commonality between the books and many instances where observations from one book can be directly applied to points made in another.

These books are written for the lay person and include definitions of key terms and ideas and many examples that help the reader make the ideas more concrete. The books are short and non-technical and are intended to spur the reader to read more about globalization outside these books and in other sources such as magazines, newspapers, journals, Internet sources, and other books on the topics. The discussion of the positive and negative aspects of the consequences of globalization, both here and abroad, will allow the reader to make their own judgments about the merits and demerits of globalization.

A brief description of each of the six books in the series follows:

Globalization and Development—Eugene D. Jaffe
Eugene D. Jaffe of the Graduate School of Business, Bar-Ilan University, Israel, and current Visiting Professor at Copenhagen Business School, Denmark, explains the key terms and concepts of globalization and its historical development. Specifically, it ties globalization to economic development and examines globalization's impact on both developed and developing countries. Arguments for and against globalization are presented. The relevance of globalization for the American economy is specifically addressed.

There are many illustrations of the concepts through stories and case examples, photographs, tables, and diagrams. After reading this book, students should have a good understanding of the positive and negative aspects of globalization and will be better able to understand the issues as they appear in the press and other media.

Globalization and Labor—Peter Enderwick
Peter Enderwick is Professor of International Business, Auckland University of Technology, New Zealand, and a long-time researcher on international labor issues. His book provides a discussion of the impact of globalization on labor with a focus on employment, earnings, staffing strategies, and human resource management within global business. Contemporary issues and concerns such as offshore sourcing, labor standards, decreasing social mobility, and income inequality are treated. The book contains many case examples and vignettes illustrating that while globalization creates

both winners and losers, there are opportunities to increase the beneficial effects through appropriate policy.

Globalization and Poverty—Nadejda Ballard

Nadejda Ballard is a professional international business consultant with clients in the United States and Europe and is an adjunct instructor for international business at Rollins College, Winter Park, Florida. In addition to her extensive experience living and working in various countries, Nadejda is also a native of Bulgaria, a developing country that is struggling with many of the issues discussed in her book.

Globalization, which is reshaping our society at all levels from the individual to the national and regional, is also changing the way we define poverty and attempt to combat it. The book includes the ideas of academics and researchers as well as those who are charged at the practical level with grappling with the issues of world poverty. Unlike other books on the subject, her aim is not to promote a certain view or theory, but to provide a realistic overview of the current situation and the strategies intended to improve it. The book is rich with such visual aids as maps, photographs, tables, and charts.

Globalization and the Physical Environment—Ho-Won Jeong

Ho-Won Jeong teaches at the Institute for Conflict Analysis and Resolution at George Mason University and has published *Global Environmental Policymaking* endorsed by both current and past Executive Directors of the United Nations Environmental Programme. His new book for Chelsea House discusses the major global impacts of human activities on the environment including global warming, ozone depletion, the loss of biological diversity, deforestation, and soil erosion, among other topics. This book explores the interrelationship of human life and nature. The earth has finite resources and our every action has consequences for the future. The effects of human consumption and pollution are felt in every corner of the globe. How we choose to live will affect generations to come. The book should generate an awareness of the ongoing degradation of our environment and it is hoped that this awareness will serve as a catalyst for action needed to be undertaken for and by future generations.

Globalization, Language, and Culture—Richard E. Lee
Richard E. Lee teaches world literature and critical theory at the College of Oneonta, State University of New York. The author believes that globalization is a complex phenomenon of contemporary life, but one with deep ties to the past movements of people and ideas around the world. By placing globalization within this historical context, the author casts the reader as part of those long-term cultural trends.

The author recognizes that his American audience is largely composed of people who speak one language. He introduces such readers to the issues related to a multilingual, global phenomenon. Readers will also learn from the book that the cultural impacts of globalization are not merely a one-way street from the United States to the rest of the world. The interconnectedness of the modern world means that the movements of ideas and people affect everyone.

Globalization and Human Rights—Alma Kadragic
Alma Kadragic is a journalist, a writer, and an adjunct professor at Phoenix University. She was a writer and producer for ABC News in New York, Washington D.C., and London for 16 years. From 1983–89 she was ABC News bureau chief in Warsaw, Poland, and led news coverage of the events that led to the fall of Communism in Poland, Hungary, Czechoslovakia, East Germany, and Yugoslavia.

Her book links two of the fundamental issues of our time: globalization and human rights. Human rights are the foundation on which the United States was established in the late 18th century. Today, guarantees of basic human rights are included in the constitutions of most countries.

The author examines the challenges and opportunities globalization presents for the development of human rights in many countries. Globalization often brings changes to the way people live. Sometimes these changes expand human rights, but sometimes they threaten them. Both the positive and negative impacts of globalization on personal freedom and other measures of human rights are examined. She also considers how the globalization of the mass media can work to protect the human rights of individuals in any country.

All of the books in THE NEW GLOBAL SOCIETY series examine both the pros and the cons of the consequences of globalization in an objective manner. Taken together they provide the readers with a concise and readable introduction to one of the most pervasive and fascinating phenomena of our time.

Dr. Ilan Alon, Ph.D.
Crummer Graduate School of Business
Rollins College
April 2005

Introduction to Globalization and Labor

Consider the following stories that describe the lives of two people working in the global economy. While they live in very different parts of the world, globalization significantly affects both their lives.

Li's Story

Li Zhang is 18 years old and has worked in the Haifong shoe factory in the Pearl River delta region of China for two years. She is one of 7,000 girls working in the factory, which is a joint venture between Taiwanese investors and the People's Liberation Army (PLA). Her day begins at 7 A.M. with the singing of the factory song and exercises. The factory is run like a military camp. Li lives in a factory dormitory with 15 other girls. The company provides food and basic health care.

Li works a 60-hour week. After the morning shift and 15-minute lunch break, she takes the regulation nap before starting the afternoon shift. Li does not venture far from the factory. Fashion and beauty shops are appearing around the factory and Li can afford to have her hair done each week. The management also provides a disco for employees.

She is paid $12 a week and each year is entitled to a return train fare. She was recruited in her home province of Hunan, some 30 hours away by train and bus. In the past two years she has returned to her village and family only once (Figure 1.1). However, her parents rely on the money she sends home to maintain the family home. One day Li hopes to open a shoe factory in her home village and to provide jobs for her fellow villagers.

Li does not really understand globalization, but she appreciates its effects. She knows the shoes she makes will end up in one of 3,500 stores in the United States. Haifong has 2.5 percent of the U.S. market. Without globalization, she would be back in her village working the family land and probably married by now. In the factory she has freedom, a secure and well-paid job, and the opportunity for advancement. But she misses her family.

Colin's Story

Colin Walker is a professor of international business at a well-known Australian university. He has an MBA from the London Business School and completed his Ph.D. at Stanford University. In Australia he receives a salary of US$80,000 for teaching two courses a year, a total of 96 hours. Of course, for much of the rest of the time Colin is busy with research and administration but he does appreciate the 25 weeks each year when students are not at the

Figure 1.1　　Many of the girls working in the large shoe factories in China are recruited from the rural areas in the interior of China. At home such girls would be working the family land alongside the rest of their families, but here they may spend as long as a year in between visits to their relatives.

university. During this time Colin does consulting work for a major U.S. multinational corporation. Apart from the money, Colin loves to travel in the company Lear jet!

Globalization has certainly affected education in Australia. In his classes Colin has the opportunity to interact with students from many cultures: Indian, Chinese, European, and Latin American as well as Australian. Colin enjoys a high level of job security, or tenure, as it is known. Provided he produces research papers and does not get too many complaints about his teaching, he can look forward to retirement with generous retirement and health benefits.

Colin drives a two-year-old BMW from his five-bedroom home in the suburbs to work and to the gym three times a week. Colin is a very fit 49 years old; he never seems to find work stressful.

Colin also embraces globalization. He is a visiting professor in Hong Kong and his university has campuses in Malaysia and Singapore. Colin flies out to teach in these locations six times a year and is paid an additional US$150 for each hour's teaching. He enjoys the travel and excellent hotels and believes that these experiences enhance his teaching and research capabilities. With his laptop computer, mobile phone, and modem he can work anywhere in the world and still keep in touch with work and home. His university also funds him to attend three international conferences a year; last year he visited Las Vegas, London, and Tokyo. But as Colin says, it is hard to live in Australia and still keep in touch with global changes!

Both these stories suggest that globalization has brought improvements to the lives of many people. This is true, but does not reveal the full picture. Consider the following report.

A Tragic Drowning

Around 3 P.M. in the afternoon more than 30 Chinese were seen heading into the bay. Wearing waterproof clothes, clutching rakes, and dragging a dinghy, they began a long, laborious search for cockles, an edible shellfish. When local fisherman headed home at dusk, the Chinese kept on working. Perhaps it was because they were being paid just $1.87 for a 9-hour shift. Cockles sell for between $935 and $3,740 a ton, depending on their quality.

By the following morning 19 of the Chinese workers were dead, drowned in the incoming tide. Police are searching for the gangmasters thought to be behind the incident. Gangmasters are believed to house and feed the Chinese in cramped and dirty conditions, moving them around the country for agricultural, food packaging, and processing jobs.

This is a tragic story that most people find shocking. Where and when did it happen? We might think in a repressive, underdeveloped country some years ago. Actually, it occurred in Morecambe Bay in northern Britain in February 2004! This tragedy is the latest incident highlighting the dangerous and exploitative conditions facing an estimated 60,000 migrant workers employed by British gangmasters. The problem is not unique to Britain. Exploited workers can be found in many countries around the world. Is this what globalization means for labor? While this case illustrates the negative aspects of globalization, the situation is, of course, much more complex.

UNDERSTANDING GLOBALIZATION

This book is designed to help you understand a significant contemporary issue that has huge implications for all of us: the impact of globalization on labor markets. Most of us spend some time in the labor market, as employers or, more generally, as employees. The time we spend working varies from short periods, for those who become homemakers, for example, to most of our life for many others. For the majority of the population, the labor market determines our standard of living in that it provides income (wages and salaries), determines the quality of our working lives (the terms and conditions under which we work), and also influences our health and social well being. Understanding labor market conditions is important to all of us.

Clearly, labor market conditions vary between countries and over time. Working conditions in a wealthy, advanced country such as the United States are likely to be a lot more attractive than those in a poor, underdeveloped country such as Bangladesh. Similarly, we believe that we are better off, and enjoying higher wages and more attractive working conditions, than our grandparents were. At the beginning of the 21st century, labor market conditions in many parts of the world increasingly are influenced by a powerful force commonly referred to as globalization. Globalization describes a process of growing internationalization of economic activity resulting in high levels of interdependency between countries and markets. This process is evident in markets for both goods and services (you may own a European car or Japanese DVD player), and for labor services (technical support may be provided by a call center in India).

The impact of globalization on labor markets is complex and controversial. It is complex because the effects of globalization are uneven.[1] As a U.S. consumer you benefit from being able to buy lower-cost shoes made in Brazil. But if you were an unemployed U.S. shoe worker who lost his job because your company could not compete with a low-cost Brazilian rival, how do you think you would feel? Globalization is controversial because it has both positive and negative effects. People who are opposed to globalization believe that we need to do more to spread its beneficial impacts. You have probably seen or read about anti-globalist protests. These people are concerned about the negative effects of globalization. Understanding the impact of globalization on labor markets is further complicated by the fact that government policy interventions can affect outcomes. For example, a government may seek to protect jobs by restricting imports of competing products from overseas, or in banning **offshoring**, the transfer of work from one country, usually, a high wage one, to a lower-cost location.

This book will explore these issues. In this chapter, we begin by examining the nature of globalization—to clarify what this term means. This is followed by a discussion of the growth and importance of globalization and the key factors driving globalization. Then we develop the implications of globalization for business competition and how this is likely to affect labor markets. In the final section we explore the key controversies and concerns relating to labor that will be addressed in subsequent chapters.

WHAT IS GLOBALIZATION?

While most writers highlight the growing internationalization of economic activity, globalization is more than simply internationalization; it is distinguished by growing integration and dependency between countries and markets. We define **globalization** as the trend towards a single, integrated, and interdependent world. It can also be defined as the breaking down of traditional barriers between countries allowing the movement of goods, capital, people, and information. What this means is that economic events in one market may affect, or be affected by, those occurring elsewhere. This is readily apparent in financial markets, where changes spread rapidly around the world. This was evident in the 1997 Asian economic crisis, when problems that arose initially in Thailand were soon experienced in Indonesia, Malaysia, and South Korea.

At the beginning of the 21st century, the links between markets are both more pervasive and more sensitive than at any time in the past. With the collapse of Communism in 1989, the majority of countries are now part of the world economy. Furthermore, former planned economies such as China or Russia are increasingly open to trade, foreign investment, the transfer of technology, and the international movement of people. The rapidity of connections between countries and markets is shown, for example, by the speed at which computer viruses are spread through the Internet. Where commentators disagree is on the scale and scope of globalization, and the nature of the interdependencies that exist.

Some observers argue that globalization is nothing new and that all we are seeing is simply the continuation of a long-standing process. They highlight the fact that between 1820 and 1992, world population increased five-fold, world income increased 40-fold, and world trade increased 540-fold.[2] When we compare the ratio of international trade to **national income**, we find levels in the early 1990s had only just returned to pre-World War I levels. International migration levels are now lower than they were in 1900, and foreign investment today is a smaller proportion of total investment in many countries than it was in the 19th century. These sceptics argue that there is nothing new about the current period, and that we are simply observing a return to trends disrupted by two world wars and a major depression.

By "the scope of globalization" we mean the nature of the processes that are linking markets. For some writers, globalization is solely an economic process that manifests itself through trade, international investment, technology transfer, and migration. For others, it is both economic and non-economic in its nature. The non-economic aspects include the global spread of science, information, and even culture. For the purposes of our discussion, we emphasize the economic impacts of globalization because these are likely to have the most significant influence on labor markets. However, this is not to deny the importance of, say, cultural transfer in management approaches that also affect labor. Think of the many U.S. corporations that introduced some form of Japanese quality management practices in the 1980s.

While it is certainly the case that globalization over the past two decades has brought high levels of internationalization, the globalization of the late 20th century is qualitatively different to globalization a century earlier. It differs in three significant ways: (1) in the speed of international exchange, (2) in the forms of integration, and (3) in the role played by private sector business, particularly large multinational enterprises.

First, developments in information and communications technologies have greatly increased the speed and lowered the cost of international exchanges. Microprocessor technologies, such as those found in cell phones and computers, allow tremendous amounts of information to be encoded, transmitted, and processed at increasingly lower costs. Between 1950 and 1990 the cost of transatlantic phone calls fell by 29 percent; for satellite calls, the drop between 1970 and 1990 was 90 percent. More people than ever have access to these technologies. Between 1990 and 2002 the number of mobile phone subscribers in the world increased from 11 million to 1 billion, while personal computer ownership increased from 120 million to 670 million. Time spent on international telephone calls increased more than 4-fold over the same period, while the number of people with access to the Internet increased almost 200-fold to 500 million.

The second distinctive characteristic of contemporary globalization relates to the ways in which countries and markets are integrated. While international trade (imports and exports of goods and services) has traditionally provided the main linkage between economies, this has been replaced in the last decade by a new international connection: international production. Under international production, firms establish production processes in overseas markets rather than producing goods in the home country and exporting these. An example is provided by the major Japanese car companies, such as Toyota, that began to establish factories in the United States in the 1980s (Figure 1.2). International economic linkages based on production are likely to be more durable than those based on trade. While two countries may reduce or divert trade between themselves, they are less likely to jeopardize a relationship based on the ownership of factories and similar facilities by private companies. We may say that the present era of globalization is distinctive from previous periods in this shift from "shallow" to "deep" integration.[3]

The third distinguishing feature of current globalization is the important role played by **multinational enterprises (MNEs)**. MNEs are large, internationally diverse firms that own or control value-adding activities such as research and development,

Figure 1.2   Toyota is one of the major Japanese car companies that began to establish production plants in the United States during the 1980s. This one in Georgetown, Kentucky, has more than 20,000 team members who are employed directly by Toyota's manufacturing division.

production, or marketing in more than one country. The largest firms, such as General Motors, Intel, Sony, and Shell, are very well known.

These very large companies dominate international economic activity. In a global economy valued at $36 trillion in 2003, almost $24 trillion, or two-thirds, was in the hands of MNEs. In some ways this figure understates the power of MNEs. While there were estimated to be some 65,000 multinational enterprises operating in 2000, the top 100 in terms of size accounted for 14 percent of the foreign sales and assets of all MNEs. These firms are very large and powerful; many are bigger than countries. For example, of the 50 largest "economies" in 2000, 36 were countries and 14 were MNEs.[4] This highlights the tremendous impact that decisions taken by such businesses, regarding what to produce and where to produce it, are likely to have on labor markets.

THE GROWTH OF GLOBALIZATION
AND ITS DRIVING FORCES

The growth of globalization is apparent from a number of indicators of economic activity. The most significant of these are trade, capital flows, foreign direct investment, strategic alliances, and migration. All of these have shown significant increases in volume, significance, and international integration in recent years. Trade has consistently grown at a faster rate than national output. Between 1950 and 2000, global **gross domestic product (GDP)**, a measure of world output, increased six-fold, while international trade expanded fourteen-fold. By 1999, international trade represented 23 percent of world GDP, compared with 6 percent in 1950. Capital flows have also increased at a phenomenal rate. Thirty years ago, average daily transactions in foreign exchange varied between $10 and $20 billion; they now exceed $1,500 billion.

The growth of **foreign direct investment (FDI)**—long-term capital flows where investors acquire a controlling interest in an overseas business—has been equally impressive. There are now many Japanese automobile manufacturers in the United States. The ratio of the total amount of FDI to global GDP has increased from 6 percent to 16 percent in the two decades from 1980 to 2000. FDI inflows as a percentage of all private sector business investment have increased from 3.4 percent to 14 percent over the same period.[5] Strategic alliances, which are cooperative arrangements between businesses, show a similar trend, with estimates suggesting a six-fold increase between 1989 and 1999. One successful example is that between Kentucky Fried Chicken (KFC) and Mitsubishi in Japan.

International migration mirrors all of these trends. Estimates suggest that 42 million people migrate temporarily for work each year, while 6 million migrate permanently. Worldwide, 130 to 145 million legally registered migrants permanently live outside their countries of origin. Global travel has also increased dramatically, with nearly 600 million people traveling internationally each year.

Understanding what is propelling the growth of globalization is made easier by distinguishing between factors that we term "facilitators," conditions that have made globalization possible or easier, and "drivers," the factors that have caused it.

The key facilitators of globalization are the information and communications revolutions, market liberalization, and the relative world peace of the period since 1945. Major technological changes in communications and computers have brought about an information-based society. By almost any measure, information and communications technology (ICT) play a more significant role in the economy. We have already presented some indications of the growing importance of ICT. The implications of these developments are dramatically lower costs, increased speed, and ease of managing business operations around the world.

Market **liberalization**, the elimination of restrictions and regulations controlling access to markets, has enabled an expansion of both trade and international production by facilitating access to overseas markets. One indication of this liberalization is the number of countries involved in trade rounds, the periodic discussions between countries that seek to reduce trade barriers. The first post-war trade round of 1947 involved just 23 countries; the Uruguay round in the mid-1990s had 123 participant countries. The average **tariff** (a tax on imported products) on industrial products among developed countries fell from more than 40 percent in 1947 to less than 5 percent in the late 1990s. Markets also have been liberalized for foreign direct investment. The United Nations notes 1,035 regulatory changes over the 1990s, of which 94 percent were more favorable towards foreign direct investment.[6]

Finally, globalization has been facilitated in the period since 1945 by the relative world peace that has existed. This has encouraged both trade and international production, as international commerce depends on relatively stable international relations.

The drivers of globalization are those forces that are propelling the closer integration of economic activities around the world. Globalization is fundamentally a business-driven phenomenon, resulting from operations that firms undertake across borders in order to organize their research, development, production, marketing, and financing activities.

In the highly competitive global era, MNEs develop strategies to maximize their competitive capability through a mix of the benefits of globalization (using differences between locations is terms of cost and factor quality, flexibility, and opportunities to learn from global markets and consumers) and the benefits of being locally responsive (understanding individual market needs, product or service adaptations, and positive host country relationships). This strategy has been pursued with great success by the global music channel MTV. The importance of international businesses in driving globalization means that it is useful to examine the sorts of competitive pressures that they experience and how they are likely to react to these. The strategic focus of an international firm has significant implications for labor markets.

BUSINESS COMPETITION IN THE GLOBAL ERA

The increased globalization of business has brought unprecedented levels of competition as markets and industries have increasingly opened up. Firms have responded to the growing competition in a number of ways, primarily by (1) seeking new sources of competitive advantage, (2) managing knowledge more effectively, (3) taking advantage of differences between business systems, and (4) adapting to accommodate increased pressures in the business environment.

First, businesses have sought new sources of competitive advantage. **Competitive advantage** refers to the distinctive skills, abilities, or resources that enable one particular organization to distinguish itself from others. This allows firms to create unique positions for themselves in the competitive landscape that is their industry. There are many sources of competitive advantage. Traditionally, many firms competed on the basis of costs. Such an advantage was typically derived from differences in labor, energy, or raw material costs. At one time, quality provided a basis for sustained differentiation but this is increasingly difficult in a time when for most consumers high quality is a given. Technology, management skills, established brand names, and exclusive access to distribution networks provide increasingly important sources of competitive advantage. The distinguishing feature of these forms of advantage is that they are labor-based: people develop and apply new technologies, create brand positions, and introduce innovative new management approaches, for example.

Second, globalization is also associated with a time when the key productive resource is knowledge. Land and capital are no longer the primary drivers of business success; rather, it is knowledge. Knowledge is unlike other resources, in that traditionally, the value of resources has been determined by their scarcity. Knowledge does not follow such a law; indeed, the more that knowledge is spread and used, the more valuable it becomes. Of course, knowledge becomes old very rapidly. Think of the value of yesterday's newspaper. But before it becomes obsolete, the more plentiful it is, the more valuable it is. If you learn something useful in school and share this knowledge with your friend, it does not reduce the value of this knowledge, but probably increases its acceptance and value. The explosion in knowledge means that considerable resources will be put to managing knowledge. Businesses can expect to gather more information from their external environment, process and apply more information internally, and direct more information to interested parties such as shareholders, consumers, and employees. The effective management of knowledge can provide a basis for the creation of a sustainable competitive advantage. Again, it is people who manage knowledge.

A third implication of the global business environment is where firms choose to conduct different aspects of their business. Globalization and the lower costs of coordinating worldwide operations have enabled companies to take advantage of the considerable differences that exist between national business systems. Such business systems can provide diversity in terms of resource quality, cost, institutional structures, and culture. Multinational businesses can exploit these differences in the location of particular business activities. For example, a firm may place research and development in the United States, assembly in China, and marketing within the U.K. Each activity is based in the best location as determined by cost, quality, geography, government policy, and the availability of appropriate skills and experience. This development has obvious implications for employment as business activities are situated around the world in what firms see as the best locations for them.

Fourth, as the global business environment becomes more turbulent and dynamic, organizations will need to adapt to accommodate the new pressures. Structural changes to improve flexibility and adaptability have involved organizational restructuring, typically a shift from large traditional hierarchical organizational structures with many layers of management, to flatter, broader structures with shorter time delays in information processing and decision making as well as empowerment of lower-level employees. Clearly, changes of this nature have an impact on employees, as layers of middle management are eliminated, the intensity of work increases, and production workers assume greater responsibilities for production scheduling, quality control, or customer service.

GLOBALIZATION AND LABOR MARKETS

Table 1.1 suggests that the globalization of business has had four principal effects on labor. First, increased competition has heightened the need for new forms of competitive advantage. This, in turn, means increased demand for creative human

Table 1.1   **The Links Between Globalization and Labor Markets**

	RESULTS IN:	EFFECTS:	RAISES CONCERNS ABOUT:
GLOBALIZATION OF BUSINESS	Increased competition and the need for competitive advantage	• Importance of knowledge and human resources. • Pursuit of new human-resource based forms of competitive advantage	• Skill levels and shortages. • Effective management of human resources. • Downward pressure on wages and conditions. • Payment for skills.
	Increased location choice and international interaction	• Levels of employment. • Security of employment. • Quality of working life.	• Job loss and relocation. • Offshoring. • Deterioration in working conditions and the power of labor. • Workplace diversity (race, age, gender, etc.)
	Demand for high-level managerial skills	• Skill levels and type of employee desired. • Training investments. • Career paths.	• Management skills and shortages. • Global sourcing of management skills. • Development of global managers. • Gender balance in the work place.
	Organizational restructuring and the pursuit of increased performance	• Levels of employment. • Security of employment. • Quality of working life.	• Job security. • Changes in skill levels. • Work intensification. • New working practices.

resources, the people who develop these advantages. Such a strategy raises concerns about the type of skills demanded and how to overcome skill shortages. Skills that are in strong demand may pay better wages, and this can disrupt wage equality. If human resources underpin competitive advantage, then the effective management (recruitment, motivation, and retention) of such people is of critical importance to the success of the firm. In many cases, high levels of competition bring down wages and working conditions.

Second, the global spread of business gives managers the ability to choose almost anywhere in the world to locate activities. This has obvious implications for levels of employment, job security, and working conditions. This is a major concern of labor and is evident from the ongoing debate regarding offshoring and labor market adjustment.

A third implication is that the effective management of global operations requires highly skilled personnel. Where these managers are found and how they are developed and rewarded will affect career paths and decisions to invest in education.

Fourth, many firms have been forced into organizational restructuring, such as eliminating layers of middle management, as a result of the competitive pressure of globalization. Again, this has significant implications for the employment situation. How employees fare in this process depends on whether work is relocated, whether machines are substituted for people, or whether new working practices are imposed (Figure 1.3).

Clearly, there are significant connections between economic globalization and labor market outcomes. We will address many of these connections in subsequent chapters.

KEY CONTROVERSIES AND CONCERNS

The remaining chapters in this book address some of the major controversies that result from the globalization of labor markets. Chapter 2 discusses the relationships between globalization and employment. Here the controversies relate to employment

Figure 1.3   In September 2004, Volkswagen warned its German workers that 30,000 jobs could be slashed if they did not agree to a wage freeze and other concessions. These measures were due to declining automobile sales and rising oil prices in the recent months. These factors put pressure on workers to work more for less pay. Here, a worker holds a placard reading, "Captain Hartz, it's a trip on the Titanic for us" during a warning strike at their plant in Hanover, northern Germany. The man he is addressing—Peter Hartz—is the head of personnel at Volkswagen.

security (as jobs are being moved from country to country), the quality of employment (working conditions), and the growth of offshoring (the shift of production and business services to lower-wage economies).

Chapter 3 examines trends in earnings during the global era. The principal controversy in this area relates to growing inequality, particularly between the highly skilled and the less skilled, and whether this can be attributed to globalization. We will consider both globalization and other factors such as technological change, which can help explain growing income inequality.

In Chapter 4 we turn to look inside the firm and the ways in which labor relations may be expected to change as a result of globalization. The principal controversy we consider in this area is whether the power of organized labor has been adversely affected by the growing importance of global economic relationships.

Chapter 5 tackles the related issue of how the management task is likely to change when operations are increasingly managed globally. The job of management is expected to become more complex and demanding. The power of collective approaches to management suggests a move towards team and project organization.

The key issue to be evaluated here is whether the nature of management work has changed and if a group of so-called global managers will emerge.

The considerable controversies that globalization has created for labor have resulted in calls for public policy interventions to try to redress the problems. This is the subject of Chapter 6. The key issues here are whether such intervention is warranted, how effective it is likely to be, and what are the best forms of intervention.

Chapter 7 provides an overview of the issues we have examined in the previous chapters. It should be apparent that these controversies are complex and involve issues that are not easy to understand. Furthermore, they are not straightforward in interpretation. Assumptions that we make about how the world works (or should work) affect our interpretations. Perhaps the most important lesson you can draw from our discussion is that these are extremely important issues that affect or will affect all of us, directly and indirectly.

CONCLUSION

This chapter has introduced the area of globalization and labor. We have suggested that this is both a complex and an important topic. It is complex because of the myriad ways in which globalization is likely to impact on labor, the difficulties of generalizing these effects, and the sensitivity of assumptions made. Nevertheless, it is an important topic because most of us will spend some time, often a lifetime, in the labor market. What we are likely to experience in the global era of the early 21st century should be a concern for all of us.

Globalization
and Employment

Having declared free trade and open borders to be America's policy, why are we surprised that corporate executives padlocked their plants in the Rust Belt and moved overseas? Why keep your plant here when you can manufacture at a fraction of the cost abroad, ship your goods back, and pocket the windfall profits that come from firing twenty-dollars-an-hour Americans and hiring fifty-cent-an-hour Asians?

—Patrick Buchanan, *The Great Betrayal*

The above quote highlights a major current concern for much of the American public: the impact of globalization on the labor market. In this chapter we will examine this concern and consider how globalization is related to the level and pattern of employment, to growing job insecurity, to changes in the quality of employment, and to the ways in which labor markets adjust.

INTRODUCTION

A recent *Business Week* editorial claimed the most important debate in the economy right now concerns the future of the U.S. labor market.[7] In large part, this debate is about how globalization is changing the workings of labor markets. The increased trade and foreign investment that result from globalization bring greater economic specialization within countries and increased competition between them. While this benefits consumers in the form of lower prices, it also changes the pattern of employment. This is nothing new; such changes, driven by trade and technology, lie behind the long-term productivity and wealth increases much of the world has enjoyed. However, it does bring changes in employment patterns, and such transitions may be difficult. In 1900, 38 percent of the U.S. work force was engaged in farming; today the farming sector produces more food while employing just 2 percent of the work force. What is new about the current concern is the range of employment that is now viewed as being under threat. While low-skill manufacturing jobs have long been exposed to competition from lower-wage economies, the threat of overseas competition now applies to a range of service and semiskilled jobs that were generally considered to be immune from such concerns.

LEVEL AND PATTERN OF EMPLOYMENT

Globalization is likely to affect both the level and pattern of employment. It affects total employment levels through its impact on growth. Countries open to trade become more specialized, their firms achieve the benefits of larger size when they have access to bigger markets, incomes rise when consumers enjoy lower prices, and openness facilitates the exchange of technology and new ideas. If, as the evidence suggests, open economies (such as Singapore) grow more rapidly than closed ones (such as North Korea), then we could expect globalization to add to overall employment. This certainly seems to be the case for the United States, which has seen increases in both its reliance on trade and employment levels. In 1970, manufacturing imports from developing countries equaled 0.8 percent of U.S. gross domestic product (GDP); by 2000, they represented 4.6 percent. There is also evidence that U.S. multinationals have transferred production and employment overseas.[8] At the same time, U.S. employment has grown. Between 1980 and 2002,

America's population grew by 23.9 percent, while employment increased by 37.4 percent. Currently, U.S. employment is 138.6 million, very high in terms of absolute numbers and as a proportion of the population.

Despite high rates of growth, a certain level of unemployment will always exist. Some people remain unemployed because they have skills that are no longer in demand and they fail to acquire appropriate new skills. Furthermore, an economy can experience **jobless growth**, as the United States did in the first half of 2004, where growth is not accompanied by employment creation. The growth may be driven by productivity increases (greater output from a given level of inputs, including labor) technological change or through automation, where machinery is substituted for labor. The Bethlehem Steel plant in Sparrows Point, Maryland, is a case in point. In the 1960s, the plant employed 30,000 workers to produce 4 million tons of steel. Today, producing the same volume of steel requires only 3,500 workers.[9]

Globalization has also brought significant changes to the structure of employment within economies. The structure of employment refers to the composition of the total work force in terms of industries and skill levels. Advanced economies such as that of the United States have experienced strong growth in demand for skilled labor but declining demand for the unskilled. This is reflected in growing income inequality between the skilled and unskilled workers (see Chapter 3), and much higher levels of unemployment among the least skilled. There is considerable debate as to whether these changes in relative demand are the result of globalization (trade and foreign investment) or of technological change. Most studies suggest that of the two, technology has had the more sizeable impact. The still modest levels of imports and the relatively small number of U.S. workers directly exposed to import competition mean that the effects of globalization are too small to explain the significant changes in employment and wages. In certain industries facing high levels of imported products produced with low-wage workers, such as textiles, clothing, footwear, and toys, it is likely that many of these jobs have been eliminated because of globalization. However, it is important to appreciate the magnitude of such effects; even at their peak in 2001, the number of all trade-related layoffs represented 0.6 percent of American unemployment.

An understanding of how labor markets operate helps to put into context the relative magnitude of these changes. Labor markets are inherently dynamic; they display constant **labor market churn** in which some workers are laid off as others are added to payrolls. It is wrong to think of the unemployed as a constant group; rather, different people are being added to, and withdrawing from, this category. Very high levels of such churning characterize the United States. During the 1990s, in a typical three-month period about a quarter of firms shed jobs, equivalent to around 8 million jobs. Yet the creation of new jobs vastly outweighed those lost; some 24 million new jobs were added over the decade from 1990 to 2000. The cumulative effect of this churning in the longer term is significant change in industry and occupational employment. For the United States, manufacturing employment has declined but has been more than offset by new jobs, particularly in service industries. In 1960, only 1 in every 25 U.S. employees was found in the business services and health-care industries. Today, the number is closer to 1 in 6.

There is emerging evidence that the dynamics of the U.S. labor market may be changing. This is apparent in two principal ways. First, economic recovery seems to be increasingly in the form of jobless growth. For example, recovery from the 2001 economic downturn in the United States created 8 million fewer jobs than would be expected from the experience of previous recoveries. This may be because technology is displacing employment (or requiring fewer new jobs), a result of a slowing of innovation rates and hence job creation, or because jobs are being outsourced. It is too early to say with any real certainty whether this growth without job creation is a change in dynamics or an exception to the historically expected pattern.

Second, the ability to move up the economic ladder appears to have slowed markedly. The opportunity to work hard, invest in one's children's education, and ensure that they have a higher standard of living appears increasingly difficult. One manifestation of this is the large number of Americans, more than 30 million, trapped in low-wage jobs.[10] People who cannot afford to invest in higher education find themselves and their children trapped. Similarly, a large proportion of immigrants, often poorly educated, have not made any real economic progress. This represents a significant departure from the popular conception of successive generations able to move upwards in economic and social terms.

The United States and other advanced economies are not alone in having lost manufacturing jobs. China has lost more manufacturing jobs in the past seven years than the United States, largely as a result of automation and restructuring. India, a country many see as attracting jobs, has experienced a decline in its formal sector, that part of the labor market subject to employment regulation, with much of the job growth occurring in the precarious informal sector that now accounts for more than 90 percent of new employment. Informal work is manifested in a number of forms including homework, street vendors, **sweatshop** production, **export processing zones** (**EPZs**), and child labor. Mexico, under the North American Free Trade Area agreement of 1994, lost some 1.3 million farm jobs in the decade ending in 2003. Along the U.S./Mexico border, the number of *maquiladora* plants (labor-intensive plants in which parts are shipped into Mexico and the finished product shipped back across the border), increased by 67 percent to more than 3,500 in seven years (Figure 2.1). However, since the year 2000, some 850 of these plants have closed, with the loss of more than a quarter of a million manufacturing jobs.[11]

Figure 2.1   Buses line up to take *maquila* workers home at the end of their shift outside the Samsung electro-mechanics plant in Tijuana, Mexico. Since 2000, many plants have closed due to the impact of the Asian financial crisis of 1997 and other downturns in the economy.

The dynamic changes that globalization brings to employment is perhaps best illustrated in the case of textiles, clothing, and footwear, one of the most cost-sensitive and global of all sectors. In 1998, worldwide employment in the industry was 29.3 million. Between 1980 and 1995, the total employment level changed relatively little. However, this disguises enormous changes at the national and regional levels. While Europe and the United States suffered large losses, significant employment gains were made in Asia.[12]

EMPLOYMENT SECURITY

Changing labor market dynamics are also generating growing concern over the issue of employment security. The focus of this discontent is less on the number of new jobs created and more on the uncertainty of existing employment. There is widespread concern that jobs will be eliminated because of trade, the transfer of technology, relocation of activities by multinational firms, and outsourcing to lower-cost economies.

The basis for these concerns is understandable. Back in 1980 nearly 70 percent of all workers in the world were sheltered from international competition by restrictions on trade and capital flows. By 2000, less than 10 percent of the global work force enjoyed such conditions. However, it is easy to overstate the size of the direct threat that workers in the industrialized economies face. Fewer than 5 percent of the work forces of America and the European Union are in direct competition with workers in low-wage countries, and many of these workers are in highly protected sectors such as agriculture.

Vulnerability to such competition also depends on the skill content and complexity of one's job. While there is much concern in the information technology (IT) industry about offshoring, it is primarily basic programming jobs—code writing, testing, and updating—that are moving overseas and those at the top end of the IT chain, systems architects who design complex IT systems, for example, face no such threat.

Concerns about employment security are not new. A decade ago, some argued that the country was in danger of losing its technological lead through the transfer of technology in industries such as semiconductors.[13] In reality, this never became a significant problem. The more substantial threat to U.S. jobs has more likely resulted from importation of foreign products made with U.S. technology, often under the control of U.S.-based multinationals. This raises an interesting issue, highlighting the possibility that the impact of trade and technology may be interactive rather than separate. Most of the studies that examine the impact of globalization on labor markets separate the effects of trade and technology. In reality, these two forces are likely to be related; when production is shifted overseas, whether through foreign direct investment or offshoring, technology forms part of the resource package. In turn, this technology can be instrumental in raising the trade competitiveness of the host country. This has happened with U.S. investment into the Mexican automobile industry, which now exports more than 70 percent of production to North America. In this way, the effects of globalization on employment may be much greater than generally assumed.

However, it is still important to recognize that productivity increases that result from technological progress, new capital investment, or reorganization of work practices are likely to be a far greater threat to employment security. The U.S. manufacturing sector lost jobs between 2000 and 2003, whereas at the same time productivity in the manufacturing sector was rising at a rate almost twice that of the overall non-farm economy.

Again, the clothing industry provides a clear illustration of the extent of the threat. Clothing imports have increased from 2 percent of U.S. domestic consumption in the early 1960s to over 60 percent in the 1990s. Since 1980, U.S. apparel employment has declined by 50 percent, with the loss of more than 600,000 jobs. The experience in Western Europe has been similar. However, we need to be careful in attributing these job losses to globalization. The assumption that not relocating production to low-wage economies would have kept those jobs in America or Western Europe may not hold. It is likely that those clothing companies faced with high labor costs would have replaced many of those people with machines.

Employment instability is not a concern that is confined only to high-wage economies; it is increasingly an issue within developing countries. Competition between developing countries to attract international investment and subcontracting work is encouraging employers in those countries to erode labor rights, to work employees more intensively, and to increase the size of the informal, unregulated sector. Economic crises, such as the one affecting Asia in 1997, also add to the uncertainty. The Philippines lost 200 garment factories following the 1997 Asian economic crisis which brought a collapse of currency values and growth in many parts of Asia.

The further elimination of regulations in industries such as clothing is likely to result in even more intense competition. The year 2004 marks the end of the 30-year-old Multi-Fibre Arrangement, which allowed industrial countries to place quotas on imports of various textile and clothing products from developing countries. With the lifting of these quotas, up to 30 million workers in a number of developing countries could lose their jobs as China and possibly India come to dominate the market. China is expected to increase its share of global clothing exports from 17 percent in 2002 to perhaps 45 percent within three years. China's competitiveness is a result of low wages, modern factories, good infrastructure (including transportation, roads, utilities, and communication networks), and access to world-class distributors in Hong Kong. Unregulated competition is likely to be disastrous for countries such as Bangladesh or Cambodia, where clothing generates more than 80 percent of all export earnings, or Vietnam, which employs 2 million apparel workers (Figure 2.2). The textile and clothing industries in these countries have few advantages and exist only because of favorable quotas. When it comes to competition, the forces of globalization do not discriminate between rich and poor nations.

EMPLOYMENT AND THE GROWTH OF OFFSHORING

In the past several years, concern over job loss and insecurity has moved beyond just trade and foreign direct investment to encompass the rapid growth of **offshore sourcing** or offshoring. This refers to the overseas subcontracting of work, usually low-skilled manufacturing and data processing, which is then exported back to the United States. The rapid growth of offshoring, and its penetration into a range of service tasks, has created considerable concern regarding the ability of the wealthy countries to create or retain such jobs.

Figure 2.2   These Bangladeshi weavers are creating women's clothes
in a factory in the outskirts of Dhaka. Over the past three decades, textile
exports have helped to lift Bangladesh out of grinding poverty. But 2004
marked the end of the Multi-Fibre Arrangement under which 47 developing
countries were guaranteed access to its main markets in the European
Union and the United States. With the lifting of those quotas, China
and India could come to dominate those markets, and this unregulated
competition could be disastrous for countries with smaller economies,
such as Bangladesh and Vietnam.

Despite the current high level of concern, offshore sourcing
is not a new phenomenon. It accelerated two decades ago with
the shifting of toy, shoe, and electronics manufacture to countries such as Hong Kong, Taiwan, and Singapore. A second, more
recent wave of offshoring has seen significant overseas relocation of services, from simple computer programming and consumer telephone call centers to IT consultancy to radiology

(X-ray) services. In the vast majority of cases, the motives are to lower labor costs and to access larger pools of skilled labor. China, India, Mexico, and various parts of Eastern Europe all have been the recipients of offshore sourcing.

The offshoring of services is still at an early stage but is expected to grow rapidly. As of July 2003, some 400,000 such jobs had moved overseas, and forecasts suggest that by 2015 perhaps 3.3 million U.S. business-processing jobs will have moved abroad. This is approximately 2 percent of the U.S. work force. Such acceleration implies growth rates of 30 to 40 percent over the next few years. Surveys of chief information officers suggest that while offshoring is currently used by less than 20 percent

Can Offshoring Explain the "Jobless" Recovery?

Until the end of 2003, the United States had been experiencing a "jobless" recovery, with employment stagnating at levels well below those in 2000. A widespread perception has arisen that a major culprit behind the dearth of jobs was offshoring, the growing practice of U.S. firms to relocate part of their domestic operations to lower-wage countries abroad. Offshoring presumably caused a reduction in U.S. output and a corresponding loss of jobs.

In fact, after the 2001 recession, U.S. domestic production rose substantially, but output per worker—productivity—jumped so sharply that instead of rising, employment declined. That is the real cause of the jobless recovery. Had GDP growth been accompanied by a continuation of earlier rates of productivity growth, there would have been some 2 million more private sector jobs than there were at the end of 2003.

When firms send work overseas, those goods or services come back in the form of imports. But a careful look at U.S. import data—especially for service imports, where most offshoring growth occurred—indicates that while the total number of jobs affected by offshoring had increased, that number was still small relative to the millions of jobs affected by the productivity surprise.

Source: Charles L. Schultze. "Offshoring, Import Competition, and the Jobless Recovery." Policy Brief #136, August 2004, The Brookings Institution. Reprinted by permission.

of large firms, this is expected to double within two years. The proportion of IT budgets spent on outsourcing has increased from around 5 percent in 1998 to an expected 40 percent in 2004. While these overall figures do not suggest an insurmountable adjustment problem, at the level of individual industries or occupations, the dislocations can be considerable. Between 2000 and 2002 alone, 87,000 U.S. computer programmers left the occupation and the unemployment rate for programmers increased from 1.6 to 7.1 percent.

The growth of offshoring reflects the considerable competitive advantages enjoyed by overseas suppliers. For example, India has some 350,000 IT workers and this number is expected to increase to over 1 million before 2008. The export earnings of India's software services market reached $6.2 billion in 2002, up from less than $500 million in the mid-1990s. India enjoys the advantages of a large pool of well-educated young workers (it graduates more science and engineering students each year than the United States), low wages, and familiarity with the English language. Because of the plentiful supply of skilled labor, India is likely to enjoy continuing low wages for the foreseeable future. As Michael Lind has stated,

> The free trade liberals hope that a high-wage, high-skill America need fear nothing from a low-wage, low-skill Third World. They have no answer, however to the prospect—indeed, the probability—of ever-increasing low-wage, high-skill competition from abroad.[14]

Indian IT firms are able to take advantage of the 10-hour time difference with the United States to offer clients the opportunity of 24-hour service. For example, when it is 9:00 A.M. in New York, it is 7:00 P.M., or the end of the working day, in Bangalore, India. They also have experience in the global delivery of IT services. Despite these strengths, Indian subcontracting firms face a number of threats. They themselves face low-cost competitors from other countries, including Indonesia, the Philippines, and Eastern Europe. The pace of offshoring may trigger a backlash in source countries. A number of U.S. states have proposed legislation to curb the offshoring of federal contracts. Despite these limits, there is a strong backlash against offshoring. Senator John Kerry, during the 2004 presidential campaign, criticized "Benedict Arnold companies and CEOs" for moving work offshore. Some 30 bills to curb offshoring by state and local governments are pending in 20 states.

Much of the controversy over offshoring results from the fact that while overall such a development may be good for the source country, these benefits disguise considerable disruption and adjustment costs at the local level. A study by the consulting firm McKinsey concluded that for every dollar of costs U.S. firms move offshore, America enjoys net benefits of $1.12 to $1.14.[15] In large part this arises from the ability to move resources (including people) from less-productive to more-productive uses. While this may be true in aggregate, the benefits do not directly compensate those who lose their jobs, spend a considerable period unemployed, or find themselves re-employed in lower-wage jobs.

It is important to recognize that a country like the United States may also be a recipient of jobs outsourced from elsewhere. Japanese automobile manufacture is an example. Exports of automobiles from Japan to the United States have fallen as companies such as Toyota, Nissan, and Honda have built up local U.S. production. Toyota is planning to produce its Camry hybrid in Georgetown, Kentucky after many years of arguing that the high quality levels demanded could only be attained in Japan. With products that benefit from being developed close to the market, or where transport costs are high, the size and wealth of the U.S. market will attract international production. This process is now becoming apparent in IT as Indian software companies invest abroad, much of it in the United States. They do this to be closer to their clients, in response to the push by big U.S. IT firms such as EDS, IBM, and Accenture into India, and to counter a threatened protectionist backlash.

There is evidence that many of the potential gains from off-shoring, in terms of cost savings, have not been realized. They have been lost both because of poor quality work by overseas suppliers and by a failure of firms to manage these contracts effectively. The McKinsey study suggests that companies need to be more proactive in the ways they use offshoring. At present, most activities that are outsourced are simply copied exactly. This results in lower-labor costs but fails to take account of the relative cost differences between the two countries. For example, labor costs relative to capital costs are high in the United States, encouraging firms to develop capital-intensive processes. For example, automobiles are produced in the United States using extensive automation (machinery) and relatively few people. The reverse is true in India. This suggests that processes that are outsourced should also be reengineered to reflect these differences. For example, X-rays sent to India for analysis are likely to be examined by medical specialists and not through an expert computer program which might be used in the advanced nations. In this way the benefits in terms of cost and reliability would be considerably larger.

Even Dilbert appreciates the challenges of offshore sourcing (Figure 2.3).

The threats to a country like the United States from off-shoring are easily overstated. First, consider that countries such as China remain low-technology producers. For example, 85 percent of China's modest exports of high-technology products came from foreign-owned firms in China. India's software industry is very much a services industry; India has only 0.2 percent of the massive and highly profitable software products industry that is dominated by Microsoft. China and India will remain low-cost and low-technology providers for the foreseeable future. One estimate suggests that despite the strong growth in demand, the wage rates of Indian software

Figure 2.3   Dilbert © Scott Adams/Dist. by United Feature Syndicate, Inc.

engineers will remain below those of the United States for at least 15 years.[16] Second, as noted previously, many offshore projects fail to deliver the potential savings they promise; this can result from poor quality, security problems, and poor customer service. Third, there are limits to the shifting overseas of many service jobs, a number of which, such as those involving education and health-care, require on-going customer contact. Fourth, companies in the industrialized countries have also developed counterstrategies. Some have tapped into new sources of labor. One firm advertised IT work within the United States, but at wage rates much closer to those of offshore competitors, and had no problem filling the vacancies. Automation offers another strategy that could eliminate much of the potential labor cost savings. Fifth, companies such as Intel and IBM are recognizing the need to upgrade their activities within the United States. While both firms are adding to their overseas employment levels, they are adding even more jobs at home. Sixth, because of these limits, some work is returning from offshore. Dell brought a number of technical-support jobs back from India to its call centers in Texas. As mentioned previously, Indian IT firms are now making significant investments in the United States.

The whole debate has become extremely heated. One characteristic of the debate that distinguishes it from earlier periods,

such as the 1980s, when the United States was widely perceived
to be losing competitiveness, is that the interests of workers and
firms are no longer seen as the same. Under offshore sourcing,
workers carry the burden, while businesses are able to lower their
costs and maintain market share. It is also interesting to note
that while the focus of this debate has been almost exclusively
on the employment effects of offshoring, very little attention has
been paid to possible wage effects. We will consider this issue in
more detail in Chapter 3.

GLOBALIZATION AND THE QUALITY OF EMPLOYMENT

As well as raising concerns regarding the security of employment,
globalization has also been associated with deterioration in
the quality of employment. This is captured in the popular
expression of "a race to the bottom."[17] This expression reflects a
view that intense international competition between developing
countries to attract investment from multinational enterprises
encourages companies to hold down wages and to ensure a cheap,
compliant work force. This results in a deterioration in both
wages and employment conditions. There is evidence of this from
countries such as Mexico, where manufacturing employment
expanded during the 1990s at the same time as real wages fell
20 percent. Industries subject to intense import-competition in
developed countries also display very low wages. For example,
full-time sewing machinists in the U.S. apparel industry are
among the lowest paid workers, with average yearly earnings of
just $16,500 in 2000.

These situations may result from interventionist government policies to increase the attractiveness of their economies
to international investors or because of a failure of firms,
industries, or countries to align themselves in a profitable way
with global markets. The experience of export processing
zones (EPZs) in the Dominican Republic and Brazil seems
to confirm this.[18] An export processing zone is a production
location in which incentives are offered to investors and

production is primariuly for export. In such cases a dispropor-tionate share of economic returns are captured by consumers, international firms, or retail buying houses.

Globalization has coincided with an apparent redefinition of work from permanent to flexible employment and from centralized sites to distance work. Indeed, some visions of the future suggest that jobs will be replaced by work; individuals with the requisite skills will find work, but few will enjoy the security and opportunities for upward progression provided by traditional careers.[19] In recent years, labor markets have become increasingly fragmented, with strong growth in the informal economy, which describes economic activities, often illegal, that are not registered or acknowledged by state author-ities and that thus avoid taxation. Such informal employment arrangements include street vendors and home workers. Informal employment has increased significantly in both devel-oped and developing economies.[20] In Latin America some 55 percent of the non-agricultural work force is found in the unregulated or informal economy. The figures for Asia range from 45 to 85 percent, while averaging nearly 80 percent in Africa. Many of these workers are women, who constitute 90 percent of workers outside agriculture in India and Indonesia and two-thirds of those in South Korea. While women workers have long been disadvantaged in labor markets in a number of ways—traditionally having lower wages, greater job insecurity, and limited unionization—these inequities are likely, on balance, to be made worse by the processes of globalization.

Home workers work either in their own home or at a fac-tory belonging to someone other than the employer. They are found in both developed and developing countries in sectors ranging from microelectronic assembly to carpet weaving. Some 90 percent of home workers are women. Home working in the United States increased between 1980 and 1990 after falling in the preceding two decades. While some workers choose to work from home for cultural or family reasons, the most vulnerable

We Have Jobs But No Dignity: The Flower Industry in Colombia

The high plains of the Savannah region surrounding Bogota, the capital of Colombia, are the heartland of a massive export industry that grew during the 1990s. Colombia is now second only to the Netherlands as an exporter of flowers. The giant greenhouses dotted across the Savannah generate around $600 million a year in export revenue. They provide half of all flowers sold in the U.S.

Approximately 80,000 women work in the greenhouses of the Savannah, tending beds of carnations and roses. On an average day, one woman will pick around 400 carnations. During peak periods, such as Valentine's Day and Mother's Day, that number can double. The flowers from a day's labor will sell in U.S. or European shops for between $600 and $800. The woman who picked them will earn a minimum wage for that day's labor of just under $2. Even with overtime payments, and working a 10-hour day, most women earn an amount that leaves them precariously close to the poverty line.

Workers have serious concerns about employment conditions and security. Compulsory pregnancy testing is common before women are granted employment contracts. In a cruel irony for an industry that generates so much profit from Mother's Day, dismissal has become a standard practice for avoiding employer-based contributions for maternity pay.

Workers in the flower industry face acute public-health risks from the use of agro-chemicals. Soils are sterilized with toxic methyl-bromide gas, and flowers are intensively sprayed with fungicides, insecticides, and nematicides. One-fifth of the chemicals used in the greenhouses of the Savannah are carcinogens or toxins that have been restricted for health reasons in the U.S. Women workers testify to spraying dichlorpropene, categorized by the World Health Organization (WHO) as carcinogenic, with no protective clothing and with only handkerchiefs to cover their mouths. Medical surveys show that two-thirds of Colombia's flower workers suffer from maladies associated with pesticide exposure, ranging from nausea and conjunctivitis to muscle pains and miscarriages.

As one worker said: '*I knew poverty before I worked in the flower industry. But it was in the greenhouses that I learned what fear and humiliation meant. Here we have jobs but no dignity.*'

Source: This material is adapted by the publisher from *Rigged Rules and Double Standards: Trade, Globalisation and the Fight Against Poverty*, 2002, with the permission of Oxfam GB, 274 Banbury Road, Oxford, OX27DZ *www.oxfam.org.uk*. Oxfam GB does not necessarily endorse any text or activities that accompany the materials, nor has it approved the adapted text.

are those working as subcontracting outworkers. Typically their work is unstable and not covered by national laws, the pay is low, few to no benefits are provided, and working conditions are poor. While the **International Labour Organization (ILO)** Convention 177 sets minimum standards for pay and working conditions for home workers and can form the basis for national wage and working conditions legislation and policies, only two countries (Finland and Ireland) have ratified the 1996 Convention.

Street vendors are found in most countries of the world, and like home workers, their numbers have increased in recent years. They are linked to globalization in two principal ways. First, many are low-skilled former employees marginalized within sectors increasingly incorporated into the world economy, such as clothing, toy making, and simple electronic assembly, and subject to intense competition, layoffs, instability, and automation. Second, as globalization encourages urbanization, street vendors increasingly provide services to the growing urban populations. Street vendors face considerable problems including a lack of legal status or recognition, harassment and eviction by local authorities, confiscation of goods, and unsanitary and hazardous working conditions.

Intense production in the informal sector is sometimes found in sweatshops, including those employing child or undocumented workers. Well-publicized cases include the use of child labor in soccer ball factories in Pakistan in 1995 and in clothing factories in Cambodia that provide products for Nike and the Gap. In both cases the adverse publicity caused these multinational firms to pull out of these countries, which lost thousands of jobs. In these cases many of the unemployed children appear to have resorted to crime, begging, or the sex trade to survive.

There are contrasting views on the utility of sweatshops. One view is that this is the way in which wealthy countries begin their industrialization processes and that such plants represent an early, but necessary step, in the development process.[21] The experience in India tends to support the first view. During the 1950s India operated as a highly closed economy and child labor was estimated to be 35 percent of the work force. Now, within a much more globally integrated economy, child labor is down to around 12 percent.[22]

The alternative view is that such factories are purely exploitative and that contemporary companies can afford to offer reasonable wages and working conditions. Greed, and the opportunity to make considerable profits, discourages them

The Struggles of Child Workers

An estimated 246 million children are engaged in child labor. Of those, almost three-quarters (171 million) work in hazardous situations or conditions, such as working in mines, working with chemicals and pesticides in agriculture or working with dangerous machinery. They are everywhere but invisible, toiling as domestic servants in homes, laboring behind the walls of workshops, hidden from view in plantations.

Millions of girls work as domestic servants and unpaid household help and are especially vulnerable to exploitation and abuse. Millions of others work under horrific circumstances. They may be trafficked (1.2 million), forced into debt bondage or other forms of slavery (5.7 million), into prostitution and pornography (1.8 million), into participating in armed conflict (0.3 million) or other illicit activities (0.6 million). However, the vast majority of child laborers—70 percent or more—work in agriculture.

Source:© UNICEF/ HQ98-0464/ Balaguer

I work in a house that has five family members. I'm the only servant. I'm very busy all day working, washing, cleaning and preparing food. The children in the family go to school, but I don't get to go. They can also watch television, but I'm not allowed. I'm not allowed to play with the children. I'm always working. I sleep on the floor in the dining room. I've never been home to visit since beginning this work. My parents came to visit me twice, and collected some money from the family, but I don't know how much.

—Salani Radnayaka, a 10-year-old girl working as a live-in
domestic servant for a family in Colombo, Sri Lanka.

Source: Human Rights Watch

from doing so. There are two problems with this alternate view. The first is that wages generally equate to productivity, and thus, lower wages in developing countries reflect lower productivity. Attempts to force up wages are likely to lead to job losses. Second, if labor were not cheaper, it is difficult to see why multinational enterprises would invest in these countries given the problems of managing global operations and the higher transport costs.

Much of the pressure on companies to improve the wages and working conditions of employees in developing countries

In Rangoon, Burma, child labor laws are virtually nonexistent, but these children hauling bricks at a construction site in 1996 are hardly alone—an estimated 246 million children are engaged in child labor around the world.

has come from consumer groups and non-governmental organization (NGOs). A number of large companies have adopted
systems of independent auditing of their plants. Problematic
labor practices are also found in export processing zones (EPZs),
which exist in more than 85 countries. Women constitute the
largest group within most EPZs. While labor practices in these
zones are more regulated than in much of the informal sector,
there are recurrent reports of low pay, limited training opportunities, and sexual harassment.

The problem of child labor remains a considerable source
of concern. The ILO estimates the worldwide number of
working children aged 5 to 17 at 246 million. Of these, some
179 million, one in every eight children in the world, are involved
in work that is injurious to their physical, mental, or moral well
being. The majority of child workers are not directly involved
in global business; most work on family farms or in the

Sewing of Soccer Balls— Child Labor in Pakistan

Media attention on children involved in the manufacture of soccer balls prior
to the Soccer World Cup in 1998 saw an ILO initiative to eliminate the
problem of bonded child labor in Pakistan, particularly around Sialkot. In
February 1998, the Sialkot Chamber of Commerce and Industry (SCCI), the
ILO, and UNICEF signed a partnership agreement that led to a local project
involving the state, a local non-governmental organization (NGO), and an
NGO from the United Kingdom. More than 3,000 children have been
enabled to stop working and attend school, while other measures have been
taken to provide their families with financial support. Since the agreement
was signed, the number of manufacturers participating in the program has
been extended to cover a wider region and include children who have been
employed to produce footballs at home. There, too, local industry, with
the assistance of international buyers, has contributed financially to
programmes of prevention, removal, and readaptation.

Source: *Labour Practices in the Footwear, Leather, Textiles and Clothing Industries.*
Geneva, 2004, p. 55. Copyright © International Labour Organization.

informal economy. Their position reflects the weaknesses of domestic laws and regulations.

Where children have been involved in international trade, publicity and consumer pressure have often brought change. In this way it could be argued that globalization has improved the plight of these children. Recent analysis suggests that the most effective way to reduce the problem of child labor is by eradicating poverty. This suggests that trade restrictions or similar sanctions on countries suspected of condoning the use of child labor may be poor policy choices, since they restrict market access, trade, and growth.[23]

Many of the problems discussed above are exacerbated where illegal workers are forced to work under debt bondage to repay traffickers who bring them into a country. The poor wages they receive and high charges (subject to mounting interest charges) mean that many individuals are forced to work for considerable periods under illegal and unacceptable conditions. Even when debts are repaid, continuing illegal status means that such workers remain vulnerable and exploited.

LABOR MARKET ADJUSTMENT

Responding to the strains that globalization brings depends, to a considerable extent, on the efficiency of labor markets and how well they adjust. The faster-growing and more competitive economies in the world tend to have flexible labor markets and decentralized bargaining over wages and working conditions. For example, differences between labor market adjustment in the United States and Europe are significant. Adjustment processes in the flexible U.S. market focus on relative wage movements rather than on enduring unemployment. The opposite is true on the European continent where wages are inflexible but unemployment is high. Indeed, there are interesting interactions between the two markets. Rising unemployment (and the withdrawal of discouraged workers from the market) among the unskilled in Europe benefits unskilled U.S. workers, whose wages fall less than they would otherwise.

The advanced countries need to upgrade their economies in terms of technology and the amount of value added to production to reduce direct competition with low-wage developing economies. This is not really anything new, as these countries have been moving in this direction for many years. The ability to generate new jobs is dependent on innovation, which requires risk-taking and experimentation.

The Ups and Downs of Job Loss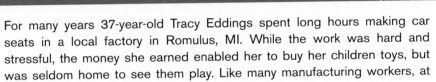

For many years 37-year-old Tracy Eddings spent long hours making car seats in a local factory in Romulus, MI. While the work was hard and stressful, the money she earned enabled her to buy her children toys, but was seldom home to see them play. Like many manufacturing workers, at night, she'd lie awake worrying about what she'd do if she lost her job.

In November 2001 her factory, Lear Seating Romulus Plant Two, closed, putting her and several hundred others out of work. Eddings, who had made $17.60 an hour, found a job as a cook at Merriman Elementary School in Romulus that paid about a third as much. Her experience is not uncommon: many of America's middle class experience lower earnings when forced to find new employment. A study by the Economic Policy Institute found that the average yearly wage of Michigan job sectors where jobs are being lost is $49,397; in growing sectors, annual pay is $36,477—a decrease of 26 percent.

Traditional measures of economic adjustment, such as unemployment figures, understate the true costs where employees find new work but at substantially lower pay rates and benefit levels.

Offsetting these costs, Tracey has found new happiness in her job. She says "money's not my biggest priority now; I feel I'm much better off." There is no stress about losing her job. She spends much more time with her husband and children. Her outlook on life has improved. Of course there have been sacrifices. Four-year-old Samantha gave up ice skating; 8-year-old Levi gave up ice hockey. The Eddings have fewer weekend getaways and dine out less. Life does not end when earnings decline, but it changes.

Source: Adapted from Ron French, "Job loss lets mom spend time with kid." *The Detroit News* (Sunday, March 7, 2004).

The general consensus is that in most countries globalization brings far greater benefits than it does costs. The most effective policies for addressing the costs are likely to be those of government spending and taxation. Expenditures should focus on education, training, and adjustment assistance. Modest progressive taxes enable equitable redistribution of benefits. Policies based on **protectionism** or the enforcement of labor standards are likely to be less effective and more costly. One estimate suggests that since the 1970s, the costs of protecting the dwindling number of U.S. steel jobs through trade restrictions, which raise prices, may total more than $1 million per job.[24] Research suggests that the U.S. labor market has coped well in adjusting to the pressures of change. Between 1979 and 1999 almost 70 percent of those who lost jobs in the non-manufacturing sector as a result of import competition were reemployed. Of these, more than half took a pay cut and 25 percent suffered a cut of at least 30 percent.[25] However, as the boxed reading illustrates, job loss is not always a negative experience.

CONCLUSIONS

In this chapter we have considered the impact of globalization on employment. We have seen that globalization affects the quantity, structure, and quality of employment. Employment security has been reduced by the growing competition between labor markets in different parts of the world. The current concern in the United States is with the growth of offshoring, which has spread from simple manufacturing to service activities. Observers are divided on the issue of whether globalization is driving a "race to the bottom" or whether it provides the first steps necessary for a "haul to the top." Managing the labor market impacts of globalization is best achieved through ensuring efficient labor market adjustment processes. Our discussion suggests a number of conclusions.

First, assessment of the impact of globalization depends on the time frame we adopt. In the short term, the forces of globalization bring temporary disruptions and adjustment difficulties; in the long term, there is little doubt that maintaining an open economy brings huge economic gains.[26]

Second, disentangling the effects of globalization is complicated by the fact that it has coincided with other significant labor market changes including a decline in manufacturing employment, falling demand for unskilled workers, growing wage inequality, and a slowdown in real wage growth. Discerning whether these changes are linked to globalization or technological change, or some combination of the two, is no simple matter. Indeed, we have suggested that trying to separate these effects may be misleading and that they are linked through overseas investment by multinational enterprises.

Third, the effects of globalization cannot be considered in isolation, in that they are partly determined by domestic policies and institutions. Protectionism will not save jobs subject to import competition. If jobs are not relocated, they are likely to be lost to automation. Where labor markets operate efficiently, competitive pressure will be reflected in price changes, in this case as changes in relative wages. If market forces are impeded and wages fail to adjust, the result is likely to be growing unemployment. Similarly, government policies can substantially change the impact of globalization, moderating negative effects, and promoting equity. We consider the relationships between globalization and earnings in the next chapter.

Globalization and Earnings

INTRODUCTION

There are two debates over the impact of globalization on earnings and wage inequality. The first relates to how globalization is expected to influence earnings. Trade with developing countries and capital flows from the advanced countries to developing economies as well as increased investments in education and learning are generally expected to reduce income differences both between and within countries. Unfortunately, trends in relative earnings do not follow these expectations. As we will see, one of the most striking developments in recent decades has been growing inequality between and within countries.

A second debate relates to the relative importance of globalization in affecting labor markets when compared with other influences, particularly technological change. A challenge to understanding the role of globalization is that it has not occurred in isolation; it has largely coincided with a period of significant technological change and the mass adoption of computer and related technologies. The relative significance of these developments, their independence, and direction of impact are all strongly contested.

In this chapter we will explore these debates and examine the impact of globalization on earnings. We begin by looking at the evidence on wages and earnings, with a particular focus on the problem of growing wage inequality. We then consider whether globalization can explain these developments, that is, the ways in which we would expect globalization to affect earnings. We then turn to the possibility that globalization may change the nature of labor markets, exacerbating problems of inequality. Finally, we evaluate the debate on the relative strengths of globalization and technological change in determining the growth of earnings and wage inequality.

TRENDS IN EARNINGS AND INEQUALITY

How we measure earnings, whether we look at pre- or post-tax levels, and how we factor in variations in hours worked all affect measures of household income. Comparisons at a global level are even more difficult when we recognize different definitions, coverage of data collection, and measurement quality. National assessments also acknowledge that earnings vary consistently with educational levels as well as with geography, that is, wages in the coastal cities of China are many times higher on average than those in the rural northern provinces of the country.

Confusion also arises when we move between absolute measures of earnings, that is, how much an individual or household receives, and relative measures, that is, how much an individual or household earns compared to other reference groups. If we are talking about the millions of very poor in Africa and South Asia, then the most important measure is probably absolute income, such as the number living on $1 a day or less.

If we are discussing why U.S. call center jobs are shifting to India or the Philippines, then we are likely to be more concerned with relative wage rates.

Understanding trends in earnings would be far easier if we could simply dissect the forces of demand and supply that impact wages. Unfortunately, things are not this simple, and earnings are significantly affected by a range of labor market character-istics, including flexibility, level of union organization, and policy interventions such as minimum wage standards. This means that we may expect marked differences in earnings trends between countries. As we will see, the experience of the United States and the United Kingdom in recent years has been quite different than that of continental Europe.

Table 3.1 summarizes the three principal measures of income inequality—cross-country inequality, global inequality, and within-country inequality—and whether these are increasing or decreasing, according to key studies.

Cross-Country and Global Income Inequality

The historical evidence suggests that in the previous era of globalization during the second half of the 19th century, considerable closing of wage gaps occurred. Thus, we might have expected further convergence in wages in the last three decades (1975–2005), when globalization has also been a strong force.

However, this finding depends on how inequality is measured. Using measures of cross-country inequality, the evidence sug-gests the income gap between countries is growing rather than decreasing. Very slow growth and economic decline in some of the poorest countries in the world mean the gap has increased. When we use measures of global income inequality, however, some studies suggest the gap is lessening. This is because of the high rates of growth enjoyed by a few of the world's most populous countries such as India and China, which have greatly lifted the incomes of many millions of people.

Table 3.1   Measures of Income Inequality

CONCEPT OF INCOME INEQUALITY	MEASUREMENT BASIS	EVIDENCE INDICATES
Cross-country inequality	Inequality in average income between countries	Divergence: Wage gap is growing
Global inequality	Income differences between individuals irrespective of country of residence	Convergence: Wage gap is closing
Within-country inequality	Income differences between groups within a country	Mixed: Increased inequality within countries such as Brazil, China, United States, but low and stable inequality in France, Japan, and Canada

Overall, cross-country and global inequality income differences among the citizens of the world are both massive and increasing. Inequality appears to have increased by 5 percent between 1988 and 1993. The richest 1 percent of people in the world (less than 50 million people) receives as much income as the bottom 57 percent (2.7 billion people) combined.

There are a number of factors that can help explain these trends. First, low growth in incomes of the rural population of much of South Asia and Africa has resulted in a growing income gap between these countries and the advanced economies. Second, the collapse of the former Eastern European bloc has pushed many people in these countries from middle- to low-income levels. Third, growing inequality within large countries such as China and India has affected global income distribution. In these countries, urban income levels have moved far ahead of incomes in the rural sector. Global inequality has grown significantly, given the numbers involved (more than 800 million in China alone).

We cannot simply attribute increasing income inequality to globalization. For this we need more direct proof of the relationship between inequality and measures of economic openness such as trade and foreign investment. Evidence on this question is available in two forms. One is provided by studies of trends in inequality within individual countries. These studies show that increasing inequality has occurred within both high- and poor-performing economies. This evidence suggests that even if economic liberalization accelerates growth, not all groups in society benefit equally.

The second type of evidence is provided by direct tests of the relationship between measures of inequality and openness. Here the evidence is mixed, with some studies suggesting that the poorest receive little benefit from globalization.[27] A possible explanation for these conflicting findings may be the influence of policy interventions in economic liberalization. Globalization may also have joint but conflicting impacts.[28] By increasing growth rates in countries such as China and India, globalization has probably reduced global income inequality by raising the incomes of those in competitive industries, but may have raised within-country inequality by widening growth rates between the competitive and uncompetitive industries or the urban and rural sectors.

Within-Country Inequality

Trends in earnings and inequality within individual countries such as the United States are much clearer. However, while the U.S. and the U.K. labor markets have both experienced marked rises in income inequality in recent years, this experience is not common to all developed economies. In particular, both countries have experienced a sharp rise in the wages of skilled workers compared to those of the unskilled. That other developed countries such as Sweden and Italy have not seen the same trend is surprising if we assume, quite plausibly, that much of the effect is due to the adoption of new technologies that has occurred in all of the advanced countries. The explanation may lie in the nature of these countries' labor markets. Both the United States and the United Kingdom are characterized by flexible labor markets. This means that changes in demand for workers will manifest themselves primarily as wage changes as opposed to the higher levels of un-employment more characteristic of some European labor markets, such as Germany and France. One suggestion is that countries such as the United States and the United Kingdom have moved both further and faster than elsewhere to introduce performance-based pay systems. This will tend to widen inequalities. An alternative explanation is that countries such as Canada and France that have not experienced significant increases in inequality have experienced rapid increases in the supply of skilled workers, reducing the advantage in wages that skilled workers enjoy.

In recent years the U.S. labor market has been characterized by three principal trends. First, there has been a decline in levels of manufacturing and industrial employment. In large part, this reflects a structural change as the United States has increasingly become a service, or post-industrial, society. Second, the growth in labor demand has been for more highly skilled workers. These first two trends have been experienced in most industrialized countries, not only the United States and the United Kingdom. Third, given that only a quarter of the U.S. work force has at least a college degree, the majority of workers have experienced slow growth in real earnings.[29] The growth has been slowest, and even negative, for those at the lowest income levels. In combination, these trends have exacerbated earnings inequality within the United States.

From 1973 to 1993, 60 percent of U.S. households experienced flat or declining real incomes. However, the experience with regard to real wage growth depended on where one was placed on the earnings distribution. Wage growth was slowest, and even negative, for those with the lowest incomes. These contrasts reflect differences in skill levels, since the most highly skilled workers enjoyed positive, if modest, real wage growth over most of the same period. It is difficult to attribute this to globalization; the growth in labor productivity and real wages has been slowest in the service sector, which is largely non-traded.

The return on skills has increased dramatically. Within manufacturing industries the wage difference between production and non-production workers increased from just over 50 percent in the early 1960s to close to 75 percent by the mid-1990s. More specific estimates for college-educated workers suggest that for college-educated male workers, the skill premium increased from 30 percent in 1979 to about 70 percent in 1995. It has been suggested that the return on an investment for a Ph.D. over an individual's working life is now 1 million dollars.

The growth of inequality in the United States occurred earlier than elsewhere, and levels of inequality are much higher than in most other countries. Because U.S. policy makers do not regulate labor market operations to the same extent as elsewhere, the United States was the only developed economy to experience a greater growth in inequality of after-tax family income than earnings.[30]

The growth of inequality might be less of a concern if mobility across the income distribution had also increased. In this way, workers in the lowest earnings groups would be able to move up over time. However, as suggested in Chapter 2, this process of upward mobility appears to have slowed down, and there is a concern that the lowest-paid now represent a largely fixed, rather than a transient, labor pool.

THE IMPACT OF GLOBALIZATION

Some insights into how globalization is likely to affect earnings are provided by trade theory. Trade theory illustrates how

countries can use their comparative advantages through trade to
raise productivity and earnings. It is useful to draw a distinction
here between the impact of globalization on income levels (the
level of income received) and on income differences (differences
in income levels between groups or individuals).

Globalization and Income Levels

Globalization might be expected to have an impact on income
levels in a number of ways. First, trade and outsourcing expands
markets for producers, enabling them to produce at greater
efficient scale with lower costs. Second, globalization encourages
the exchange of technologies and ideas, increasing productivity
and hence incomes in local economies. Third, reductions in
barriers to trade and investment should lower costs, and if
these are passed on, consumers enjoy greater consumption and
improvements in their purchasing power. Fourth, globalization
provides the opportunity to exploit differences between locations
in factor costs and quality and to increase specialization. All
of these benefits should in theory contribute to faster growth,
higher productivity, higher earnings, and hence higher incomes.

Globalization and Income Differences

Trade theory suggests that globalization will affect relative
incomes through the exploitation of **comparative advantage**
in different locations. In relative terms, skilled labor is more
abundant in advanced economies, while unskilled labor is more
abundant in developing countries. Developing countries with
plentiful supplies of low-skilled labor will attract production and
specialize in labor-intensive low-technology goods and services.
This will reduce the demand for unskilled labor in the developed economies, while increasing demand and wages for such
workers in developing countries. Globalization could thus result
in increased inequality within developed economies or increased
unemployment if labor markets prevent downward adjustment
in the wages of unskilled workers. When outsourcing is included,

the effects on inequality are likely to be much greater. In this situation, multinational firms move the least skill-intensive processes offshore, greatly reducing the demand for unskilled labor in the source country. At the same time, globalization should reduce inequality within developing countries.

The degree to which changes in relative incomes can be attributed to globalization depends critically on the extent of overlap between the labor markets of developed and developing countries. The comparatively low level of **import penetration** in industrialized countries suggests that trade alone probably does not provide an adequate explanation. For example, in the year 2000, imports from non-Organization of Petroleum Exporting Countries (OPEC) developing countries were equivalent to only 3.9 percent of the gross domestic product of the industrialized economies. Only about 4 percent of U.S. manufacturing workers and 5 percent of the European Union work force compete directly with workers in developing countries.

Figure 3.1 summarizes the principal routes through which relative wage changes can occur. Changes in demand, for example, a shift in spending from consumer electronics to health-care services, will change the demand for different types of labor and hence will have an impact on earnings. Since such changes are generally gradual, that this has probably not been a major factor. Second, as discussed previously, international trade affects the demand for labor and in the developed countries this should favor skilled over unskilled labor. Third, technological change obviously has a direct effect on employment opportunities and thus, wages. We will return to this factor in more detail later.

On the supply side, population growth, immigration, and the number of people undertaking advanced education and training will affect relative earnings. Population growth has not been particularly strong in most of the developed economies and cannot explain the sizeable earnings shifts observed. Immigration has probably had a more significant effect, particularly in the United States. Recent U.S. immigrants, especially those from

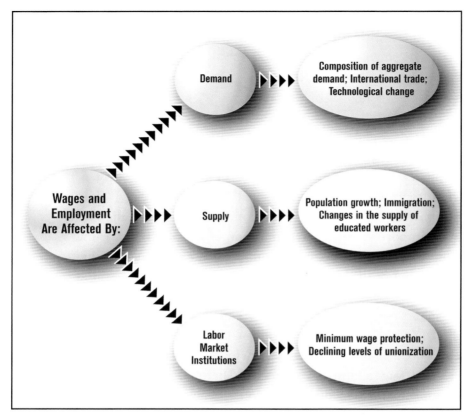

Figure 3.1   Relative earnings are affected by a variety of factors, including how many people undertake advanced education and training. Technological change has a rather obvious effect in that it can make some skills highly sought after while others may become less in demand.

Mexico, have lower levels of qualifications than those who entered the country during the 1960s and 1970s. Immigration, by adding to the supply of unskilled labor, could have contributed to the falling relative earnings of the least skilled. On the other hand, the growth in the number of workers with a college education should have reduced the skill premium. The number of highly skilled workers (those completing college) has increased in the United States from 11 percent of the labor force in 1970 to 25 percent in 1999. This increase in the supply of skilled workers should theoretically lower the wage of skilled workers. The fact that the skill premium has increased suggests that the demand for skilled labor, perhaps because of technological change, has outweighed increases in supply. We also need to recognize that changes in labor market institutions such as unionization levels and minimum wage policies can also influence relative earnings. We consider these issues in more detail later in Chapter 4.

Inequality and the Nature of Globalization

It is also worth noting that the impact of globalization on earnings depends not just on the extent of globalization, but also on a country's terms of involvement in the global economy. This is an issue of particular importance for developing countries. This problem reflects the more general concern that the benefits of globalization are enjoyed by some, but not by all. Critics suggest that the international business system follows rules that favor the wealthy countries at the expense of the developing world. For example, developing countries exporting to developed economies face tariff barriers four times higher than those facing trade in the other direction. This costs developing countries $100 billion a year, twice what they receive in foreign aid.

Developing countries, it is argued, face four types of inequity in the trading system. First, they face barriers to market entry. These may be in the form of tariffs, non-tariff restrictions, or discriminatory trade agreements. Second, these countries are overly dependent on commodity products such as cocoa beans and rubber, the prices of which are often low and unstable. Low prices adversely affect the terms of trade of commodity-exporting countries, meaning that they have to export more to pay for a given amount of imports. Third, the globalization of production under the auspices of multinational enterprises is subject to limited regulation, much of which is voluntary. The problems that can arise from this were discussed in Chapter 2. Fourth, the rules that underpin the international trading system with regard to investment, services, and intellectual property, for example, particularly those set by international institutions, are seen as favoring the already wealthy nations.

These inequities impose huge costs on developing countries. For every $1 generated through exports, the low-income countries account for only 3 cents. Some idea of how this inequity arises can be gained by examining the cost breakdown of a sports shoe produced in Indonesia (Figure 3.2). For a sports shoe retailing at $100 in the United States, wages to production workers amount to a mere 40 cents; indeed, only $12 of the total price is retained by the manufacturing plant in Indonesia.

If developing countries could increase their export share by just 5 percent, this would generate for them an additional $350 billion a year, more than seven times what they receive in

The Poor Appear to Welcome Globalization

A worldwide poll conducted by the Pew Global Attitude Survey found that not only was the attitude towards globalization generally positive but there was more positive enthusiasm for foreign trade and investment in developing countries than in rich ones. For example, David Dollar writes, "in Sub-Saharan Africa, 75 percent of households thought that multinational enterprises had a positive influence on their country, compared to only 54 percent in rich countries." A close look at the economies of these countries shows why: the fast-growing economies of the world in this era of globalization are developing countries that are aggressively integrating with the world economy. Of the 38,000 people in 44 nations surveyed, those in the developing world generally blamed their local governments, not globalization, for their country's ills. Dollar also writes,

> Notwithstanding the positive views of globalization in the developing world, the survey shows that there are common anxieties around the world concerning the availability of good jobs, job insecurity, old age support, and other quality of life issues. Interestingly, people tend not to blame globalization for lack of progress in these areas, but rather poor governance in their own countries.

Source: D. Dollar. "The Poor Like Globalization." *YaleGlobal* (23 June 2003).

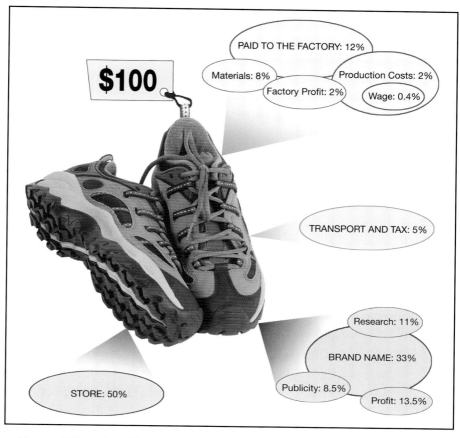

Figure 3.2 An athletic shoe made in Indonesia and retailing for $100 in the United States will net only 40 cents in wages to the worker who makes it. All the costs involved in calculating a selling price of $100 are labeled in this illustration.

aid. As suggested previously, trade is likely to be a far more effective engine of development than foreign aid. Sub-Saharan Africa provides a graphic illustration of the costs of export failure. The region's share of world exports has fallen to a third of what it was twenty years ago. The result is an average per capita income that is half of what it would have been if the trade share had been maintained at the 1980 level.[31]

The experience of countries such as Hong Kong and Mexico helps to illustrate why globalization, contrary to expectations, has brought greater income inequality. Capital inflows have tended to increase the relative demand for skilled, rather than unskilled labor, increasing the relative wages of these groups in both the host and source nations.[32] At the same time, mass migrations, continuing high levels of unemployment, and the dismantling of labor market protection in a number of countries has greatly increased labor supplies and wage competition. An interesting example of how globalization can bring greater inequality is provided by the maritime industry (Figure 3.3). Continuing concern about the links between globalization and inequality has recently resulted in a major report urging greater equity within the processes of globalization.

Globalization and Technological Change

Considering the evidence and ideas just discussed, it should be apparent that explaining rising wage inequality in terms of globalization is no simple matter. The increased supply of skilled labor in most of the advanced economies should have narrowed the skill premium, globalization of trade and investment is believed to narrow inequality between countries, and the growth of trade between developing and developed countries does not appear to have been large enough to explain the sharp rise in inequalities, particularly during the 1980s. This has prompted the search for alternative explanations, the most popular of which is technological change, particularly the adoption of computer and related technologies, which has strongly increased the demand for skilled labor. According to this view, the demand for skilled labor has outweighed the increased supply of educated employees, raising the skill premium. At the same time, work being relocated to developing countries has a higher skill content than is often believed, meaning that demand for their work and the wages of unskilled workers in these countries fall. This contributes to growing between-nations inequality. At the same time, wages of skilled workers in both developed and developing countries rise, exacerbating within-country inequality.

Figure 3.3 Historically, shipping vessels have been owned and registered by nationals of the same country that provided crews for them. This ship in the port of Bangkok is registered in Liberia—a nation that allows ship owners from other countries to register their ships. Such vessels are typically part of a fleet where the crews have no regulations protecting the workers right to unionize or to engage in collective bargaining. Competition from these open registries has brought greater inequality in wages and working conditions to those working the ships of the world fleet.

Studies suggest that globalization explains only a part of the increase in income inequality. One careful review of the studies concludes that globalization explains around 20 percent of the growing wage inequality in the United States during the 1980s.[33] Perhaps a further 20 percent can be attributed to the decline in unionization levels.[34] This means that some other factor—generally thought to be technological change—explains most of the rising inequality. However, treating globalization and technological change as independent explanatory factors may be a mistake. Rather than being separate factors, they are likely to be related. Trade and foreign investment are primary means for the transfer of technologies from advanced to developing countries. At the same time, trade may encourage investment in labor-saving technologies. This is apparent from the view that if labor-intensive work is not shifted offshore to lower-cost locations, those jobs may well be lost to automation. If this is the case, and globalization and technological change should be seen as interdependent factors, existing studies, which fail to consider these secondary effects, understate the impact of globalization on earnings inequality.

Creating a Fairer Global World

The World Commission on the Social Dimension of Globalization released its report, "A Fair Globalization: Creating Opportunities for All," in February 2004. The report supports a process of globalization with a strong social dimension based on universally shared values and respect for human rights and individual dignity, one that is fair, inclusive, democratically governed and provides opportunities and tangible benefits for all countries and people. The report emphasizes:

A FOCUS ON PEOPLE.
The cornerstone of a fairer globalization lies in meeting the demands of all people for: respect for their rights, cultural identity, and autonomy; decent work; and the empowerment of the local communities they live in. Gender equality is essential.

A DEMOCRATIC AND EFFECTIVE STATE.
The State must have the capability to manage integration into the global economy, and provide social and economic opportunity and security.

SUSTAINABLE DEVELOPMENT.
The quest for a fair globalization must be underpinned by the interdependent and mutually reinforcing pillars of economic development, social development, and environmental protection at the local, national, regional, and global levels.

PRODUCTIVE AND EQUITABLE MARKETS.
This requires sound institutions to promote opportunity and enterprise in a well-functioning market economy.

CONCLUSIONS

This chapter has examined the impact of globalization on earnings. Our discussion leads to a number of conclusions. First, it should be apparent that this is a complex issue that is not easy to understand and measure. The expectations suggested by trade theory are not supported by earnings trends. The benefits of globalization seem to have been largely captured by the more skilled workers within both developed and developing countries. Furthermore, countries like North Korea, which is not part

FAIR RULES.
The rules of the global economy must offer equitable opportunity and access for all countries and recognize the diversity in national capacities and developmental needs.

GLOBALIZATION WITH SOLIDARITY.
There is a shared responsibility to assist countries and people excluded from or disadvantaged by globalization. Globalization must help to overcome inequality both within and between countries and contribute to the elimination of poverty.

GREATER ACCOUNTABILITY TO PEOPLE.
Public and private actors at all levels with power to influence the outcomes of globalization must be democratically accountable for the policies they pursue and the actions they take. They must deliver on their commitments and use their power with respect for others.

DEEPER PARTNERSHIPS.
Many actors are engaged in the realization of global social and economic goals—international organizations, governments and parliaments, business, labour, civil society, and many others. Dialogue and partnership among them is an essential democratic instrument to create a better world.

Source: *A Fair Globalization: Creating Opportunities for All. Final Report of the World Commission on the Social Dimension of Globalization*, Geneva, February 2004. Copyright © International Labour Organization.

of the world economy, or Indonesia, which is not efficiently integrated within the global economy, have seen their relative incomes slip further behind.

Second, globalization has both direct and indirect impacts on labor markets. Directly, globalization tends to increase the demand for labor and, to a lesser extent, earnings in developing countries, while unskilled workers in the developed countries have experienced declining demand and real wages over a long period. Whether the latter is the result of globalization or technological change is a debated issue. Indirectly, globalization may depress the power and earnings of workers through the growth of the informal sector, encouraging more women to enter the labor market and increasing the **elasticity of demand for labor**.

Third, much of the growth in inequality can be explained by skill effects. The return on investments in education and training appear to have increased sharply in recent decades. Again, whether the primary cause of this is globalization or technological change is hotly debated.

Fourth, the institutional features of labor markets and their flexibility strongly influence the impact of globalization. Where markets are flexible—the United States and the United Kingdom—we observe greater income inequalities. Less-flexible labor markets are characterized by higher levels of unemployment. Recent work has proposed a linkage between these differing outcomes. In particular, in the face of increased Asian competition, when European markets experience rising unemployment, unskilled workers may withdraw from the market or reduce hours worked, lowering the global supply of unskilled labor. This benefits comparable U.S. workers whose wages fall less than they would otherwise. In this sense, the European work force is carrying some of the costs of U.S. adjustment.

Fifth, current estimates of the impact of globalization on earnings inequality appear to considerably understate the true size of the effect. This is because these models incorporate only trade in final goods, not intermediate goods (components and inputs into further production); fail to capture the effects of globalization on technical change; and ignore changes in labor demand elasticity.

Because of these deficiencies, we are left with an explanation of rising inequality based on technological change. However, such an explanation has its weaknesses. It is difficult to reconcile similar rates of technological change across the advanced nations with marked differences in the growth of inequalities within these countries. Furthermore, technological change, particularly change as radical as that associated with computerization, would be expected to raise productivity and, hence, real earnings. However, as we have seen, this does not seem to have been the experience of the majority of the U.S. work force.

Globalization and Labor Relations

INTRODUCTION

In this chapter, we shift the focus from the broad impacts of globalization on employment and earnings to examine labor relations practices within global firms. As suggested in Chapter 1, large multinational enterprises (MNEs) are now the dominant business force in world markets. These firms cross national borders, managing operations in a range of countries. There are estimated to be around 65,000 multinational enterprises controlling more than 860,000 foreign affiliates. Outside their home countries these firms employed more than 53 million people. Clearly, they have the potential to significantly impact world labor markets. The ways in which they manage their labor relations practices are of considerable interest. The labor relations practices pioneered by some of the world's leading MNEs are followed closely by other businesses. The size of these firms ensures their high profile. In 2002, the top 100 MNEs employed more than 14 million employees, of which half are within foreign affiliates. This means that on average they employ 140,000 workers, making them very sizable enterprises.

In this chapter we will first consider some of the reasons why we might expect labor relations practices within MNEs to be distinctive. We then look at the attitude of these firms towards unionization and their approaches to bargaining, decision making, information disclosure, and the transfer of innovative labor practices. Then we examine the widely discussed contention that MNEs enjoy an overwhelming advantage over labor in a global economy.

LABOR UTILIZATION AND RELATIONS PRACTICES

The globalization of business activity affects labor relations practices in a number of ways. With globalization, management tasks become increasingly complex. The human resource management function takes on a wider range of activities, perhaps becoming involved in international compensation or taxation issues. The management perspective becomes more global. Management tasks are colored by involvement in a more diverse environment, one that requires awareness of and sensitivity towards differences in languages, cultures, politics, and legal systems. It is likely that separate policies have to be developed for different groups, perhaps based on distinctions between **home-country nationals** (also called parent-country nationals), **host-country nationals**, and **third-country nationals**. For example, an American company in China may employ managers who are American (home-country nationals), Chinese (host-country nationals), and German (third-country nationals). Such diversity could create problems if people doing similar work in the same location receive different wages and conditions.

In the area of labor relations, there are several reasons to expect differences between international companies and locally owned firms. The larger average size of foreign affiliates (when compared with their domestic competitors) affects a range of labor practices that appear at least in part to be a function of size. These include union recognition, bargaining structures, and the centralization of decision making. Labor relations practices are also subject to the influence of parent-country values and practices. Despite conscious efforts to the contrary, management in foreign affiliates is invariably influenced by tradition, custom, and experience generated elsewhere in the organization.

The high levels of competitive pressure that firms face in global industries mean that we might expect MNEs to make very effective use of their labor resources. There is considerable evidence that MNE subsidiaries enjoy a productivity advantage over their domestic competitors.[35] Such comparisons are far from straightforward, as there is a tendency for foreign-owned plants to be concentrated in the more progressive and technologically advanced sectors such as pharmaceuticals and software. Similarly, these plants are often much larger than their domestic rivals, and size bestows considerable productivity advantages.

In part, this productivity advantage may be the result of more intense labor utilization, that is, working people more intensively and effectively. There are grounds for expecting labor utilization practices within MNE subsidiaries to differ from those of domestic firms. First, as suggested above, parent-country values and practices will influence approaches. A culture of cooperative labor relations management, as practiced in Germany, is quite different from the more adversarial approach of the United States. German managers are expected to consult with employees, union representatives, and supervisory boards. American managers enjoy far more independence in decision making. This will influence the approach of expatriate and parent office managers to local operations, in some cases encouraging the transplant of parent-country practices.

Second, the multinational structure of international firms may also influence labor utilization practices. When key decisions are centralized, responsiveness and flexibility may suffer. Where production operations are globally integrated, the firm can become vulnerable to multinational collective bargaining attempts, which carry high disruption costs such as strikes. Such firms may seek to avoid union organization or may attempt to "buy" peaceful relations by offering wages and conditions at least as good as those achieved by unions.

GLOBALIZATION AND UNIONIZATION

In many workplaces, the interests and well being of employees have traditionally been protected through their collective organization into trade unions. Unionization has been seen as a counterweight to the overwhelming advantage that employers, who control employment opportunities, wages, and working conditions, enjoy. While levels of unionization, at least in the United States, have been declining for a number of years and sharp decreases have coincided with the growth of globalization, it is difficult to single out globalization as the cause of this decline. In part this is because the U.S. experience has not been shared in all other advanced economies. Indeed, in a number of small, open, and globally integrated countries such as Finland, Spain, Denmark, and even Canada, union density (the proportion of the work force who are union members) has actually increased in recent years.

In 2000, the percentage of the American work force belonging to a union fell to 13.5, the lowest level in 60 years. Unionization peaked in the 1950s, reaching 35 percent, but fell to 20 percent by 1983. The sharpest falls have been among private sector workers (those not employed by the federal, state, or local government), where the unionization rate is now only 9 percent. Much higher levels, around 37 percent, exist in the public sector, the part of the economy controlled by federal, state or local government. More detailed analysis of the decline reveals that the fall has been sharpest among the least well-educated workers, with unionization levels among those with 12 or less years of education falling from 29 to 14 percent between 1977 and 1997. As we saw in Chapter 3, these are also the workers who suffered the most in terms of wage decreases. The union wage premium for these workers fell from 58 to 51 percent over the two decades to 1997, in contrast to a modest rise for better qualified union members.[36] In this way, the benefits that unions provide to workers declined the most for those in the greatest need.[37]

Determining whether these changes result from globalization, or whether they have simply occurred at the same time, is no easy matter. Plant closures due to globalization have certainly occurred at unionized companies, and these companies tend to have higher-cost operations because of union-determined wage and benefits agreements. Furthermore, many of the sectors directly involved in global competition, such as steel and labor-intensive manufacturing, have historically had high levels of union organization. It has also been argued that it is more difficult to introduce significant changes such as automation, new working practices, or technological upgrading in unionized plants. For this reason, companies may be more inclined to close or relocate rather than restructure unionized operations. However, while this may suggest an association between globalization and declining unionization, it does not necessarily imply causation.

Studies that have attempted to explain declining union membership suggest that a number of factors are at work. Foremost among these are structural and demographic trends. Structurally, the United States and other advanced economies have experienced long-term shifts in employment away from traditionally union-organized sectors such as manufacturing and mining and towards services. In the past four decades, service sector employment has increased by more than 180 percent, a rate some nine times higher than for the goods-producing sector. Service-based firms tend to be smaller on average than manufacturing facilities, increasing the costs to unions of organizing these new establishments. At the same time, many of the new jobs have been created in the South and the West, which do not have as strong a history of union organization as the northern and eastern United States.

Demographically, the composition of the U.S. labor force has changed dramatically. This is important because sex, age, and race all have an impact on union status. The growth in women's labor market participation, and in particular of women with children, has been significant. Increased female participation has also brought more part-time and home-based workers, both of which are difficult for unions to organize.

Unions also face increased competition from alternative institutional and legislative arrangements. Employment legislation makes it possible for a worker to seek individual redress in the face of unfair dismissal, discrimination, harassment, or unsafe working practices. Public welfare provision has now largely replaced what was formerly union-provided support. When these changes are combined with the pressures of increased international competition and a declining union wage premium, it may be that unions offer less and have therefore become less attractive to potential members.[38]

It appears that declining unionization levels, certainly in the United States, are primarily the result of demographic and structural changes. This would be consistent with a decline that began in the 1960s, before globalization became a major force. Like the wage issue, we can be confident in saying that globalization may have contributed to declining unionization levels, but does not appear to be the major determining factor. However, it is worth noting that the forces of globalization seem to have been more significant in affecting unionization levels of the less well educated when compared with the experience of all workers.[39]

This suggests that it will be very difficult for U.S. unions to reverse recent trends. After taking into account layoffs and retirements, in order to reverse the trends, unions would need to attract between 500,000 and 1,000,000 new members each year. While the AFL-CIO (American Federation of Labor-Congress of Industrial Organizations) has been actively seeking to recruit new members, in the longer term, there may be a need for a radical change in union strategy to increase their appeal to the overall work force.

Unions face considerable challenges within both society and individual workplaces. Global competitive pressure and the shift towards individualism have threatened traditional approaches to managing work relations. Declining union membership has thrown into question the validity of unions as a social partner in the political arena, one that advises and is consulted by government. At the same time, a number of employers, such as McDonald's, Wal-Mart, and Borders, have successfully circumvented union organization through direct communication with their work forces and the development of new collective bargaining processes separate from union channels (Figure 4.1).

Within the workplace, unions also face mounting challenges in identifying and attracting new members. An employment relationship wherein a full-time employee enjoys considerable tenure with a specific employer is increasingly rare. Part-time, short-term, and more casual forms of employment are now widespread.

For trade union organizers, globalization has created two major future scenarios. The first, pessimistic from the labor viewpoint, is that global competition will encourage the development of liberal labor markets within which traditional trade unions become outmoded by their inability to organize non-standard employment forms (part-time workers, home-workers, and contract employees) and by increased employer unilateralism as they increasingly determine wage levels and working conditions. Under such a scenario the union response is likely to focus on legislative and political regulation of the workplace. The alternative view, and an optimistic if demanding one, is that

Figure 4.1 Unions face many challenges to recruiting new members. Large corporations, such as McDonald's, have gone directly to their employees and developed new collective bargaining procedures that avoid traditional union channels.

workplace relations will shift to a more cooperative basis. This would probably mean a move towards increasingly individual-ized bargaining, emphasizing pay-for-knowledge, skill premiums, and profit sharing. The union role would focus on ensuring cooperation, enhancing flexibility, and contributing to skill development. While the latter scenario may be more attractive from the union perspective, both necessitate a fundamental strategic shift for labor unions.

BARGAINING PRACTICES

The bargaining process refers to the setting of wage and work-ing conditions determined through the coming together of employers and employees (or their representatives in the form of a trade union). Outcomes in the bargaining process depend

Cooperative Labor Relations at Boeing

After many decades of embattled labor relations, things are beginning to change at Boeing. The new CEO has negotiated with the largest union, the International Association of Machinists (IAM), for them to play a greater role in shop floor management. While in recent years Boeing has sought union concessions in making layoffs and in outsourcing work, this new initiative goes much further.

The union is supporting a High Performance Work Organization (HPWO) initiative that gives workers increasing responsibility for con-tinuous productivity improvements. It has proved highly successful at Harley-Davidson and International Specialty Products, a manufacturer of chemicals and pharmaceuticals, in boosting innovation and productivity. One of the most interesting aspects of the HPWO initiative is that it was originally developed by the IAM and was not simply a management initiative.

Boeing, which has suffered from the downturn in the global aviation industry since Sept 11, 2001, and which now faces extreme competitive pressure from European-based Airbus, needs to boost productivity by 3 to 5 percent annually to remain competitive.

Source: Adapted from "Boeing: Putting Out the Labor Fires." *Business Week* (Dec. 29, 2003): 33.

on the relative bargaining power of the two parties. Globalization may have weakened the bargaining power of labor relative to multinational employers. If this is the case, we might expect to see a fall or slowdown in the growth rate of wages and benefits; employees bearing a larger share of the non-wage costs (medical and similar benefits) of the workplace; a decline in industrial disputes; and greater instability in earnings and hours worked. We have previously noted that a number of these things seem to be occurring.[40] Multinational enterprises have long been associated with single-employer bargaining arrangements, even in those countries where multiemployer patterns are the norm. Indeed, they have pioneered practices, such as linking pay increases to productivity gains, that have now been widely adopted. Single-employer bargaining provides considerable

A Boeing 747 being manufactured at the plant in Everett, Wahington.

flexibility advantages to management, allowing a more efficient utilization of labor, more effective control of labor costs, and discretion to negotiate the elimination of impediments to productivity and change.

While multinational enterprises are often large and formally structured, there is evidence that their subsidiaries adopt bargaining arrangements that are generally compatible with local conditions. However, one area of concern to labor has been a belief that management within MNE subsidiaries are much more likely to engage in upward consultation with higher-level management elsewhere in the organization during the bargaining process. Similarly, within multiplant MNEs, management displays a high probability of engaging in consultation with colleagues in related plants.[41] Such findings are consistent with the concern of organized labor that a multinational business structure may bring insensitivities or obstacles to the bargaining process.

DECISION-MAKING PROCESSES

Multinational businesses enjoy opportunities for the centralization of key decision-making processes. The evidence suggests two clear tendencies. The first is that labor relations practices appear to be the most decentralized functional area within MNEs. This means that compared with other functions such as marketing or research and development, labor relations is more likely to be the responsibility of local plant-based managers. Second, the degree of decision-making centralization is generally higher within multinational than multiplant domestic firms and takes place at a higher level within the organization structure. This can result in protracted and secretive decision making, a charge alleged by a number of labor organizations. Furthermore, managers of international businesses have increasingly been held accountable for practices not just within the plants that they own and operate, but also within their suppliers' operations (Figure 4.2).

Figure 4.2   This worker is washing and weighing green bananas at a Dole processing plant in Guayaquil, Ecuador. Dole owns only 1 percent of the total banana-producing land in Ecuador. Dole along with Chiquita and Del Monte do not own all the land there, but buy bananas through a variety of contracts with locally owned producers. Workers in the industry and human rights monitors claim that Dole and other companies contract directly with these producers, but fail to use their influence to protect workers' rights. Thus, international managers have increasingly been held accountable for practices not just within their own plants, but also for the labor practices of their suppliers.

INFORMATION DISCLOSURE PRACTICES

An area of consistent labor concern has been the information disclosure practices of MNEs. This concern focuses on four aspects of information disclosure: (1) the level of aggregation of information provided, whether it relates to plant, division, or corporation performance; (2) the type of information disclosed; (3) the timing of disclosure; and (4) the reliability of information.

The corporate level is the usual one for the publication of external information such as company accounts. However, for many MNEs, a preference for plant-based bargaining questions the usefulness of such information. Regarding the type of information provided, MNEs display a preference for disclosing financial and operational data and a greater reluctance in providing information on labor needs and related issues. Concern over the timing of information disclosure focuses on the fact that events often precede the provision of information on those events. This is of particular concern in the case of layoffs, plant closures, reorganization of production processes, and product changes. The reliability of information is affected by national differences in the reporting forms and accounting standards. Similar problems arise when companies choose business structures such as strategic alliances, where organizational boundaries and responsibilities may be difficult to discern and the performance of individual partner firms is unclear.

INNOVATIVE LABOR PRACTICES

One effect of globalization has been to highlight performance differences between plants. This has triggered a desire to transfer "best practices" throughout the organization. Three distinct waves of innovative practices can be detected: corresponding to the expansion of U.S. MNEs in the 1960s, to the increasing influence of Japanese MNEs in the late 1970s, and the search for global best practices most recently. The competitive pressures of globalization have meant that the focus of these practices has been improvements in quality, productivity, and more effective utilization of labor. MNEs have been at the forefront in the reassertion of managerial control in the workplace. Japanese MNEs have pursued strategies focusing on single union recognition, employee flexibility through cross-training, and strict workplace discipline. The most recent wave of "best practices" has emphasized three key benefits: the use of flexible, integrated technologies; the attainment of higher standards of quality and flexibility; and a new set of relations between firms and their suppliers, generally based on trust and cooperation. Multinational enterprises such as Xerox and Hewlett-Packard have been at the forefront of these innovations.

LABOR'S POWER IN A GLOBAL ECONOMY

The labor relations practices pursued by global corporations have led to allegations that these companies enjoy an overwhelming bargaining advantage over labor. The sources of this advantage include the perceived ability of MNEs to source globally and switch production locations in the face of rising costs or difficult labor relations, the limited impact of strike action on affiliates, the extensive skills and experience of management negotiators with MNEs, and centralization of decision-making authority. At the same time, global competition in both product and labor markets has reduced labor's bargaining strength and increased vulnerability to sharp changes in wages, employment, and hours worked.

The first source of bargaining advantage concerns the possibility of relocation of production facilities. While actual shifts in facilities reduce labor demand and job security, the threat of closure may be deployed as a bargaining tactic. The distinction between threatened and actual closure is an important one. As with all forms of threat, credibility depends on its occasional exercise. The threat of closure appears to be quite widespread in the face of union drives. Recent U.S. research suggests that between 1993 and 1995 employers threatened plant closure in 50 percent of all union certification elections, a first step in establishing a union, and 15 percent actually shut down plants within two years of a successful union certification campaign.[42] The percentage of threats was much higher (62 percent) in internationally mobile industries such as manufacturing and transport, warehousing, and distribution. Mexico was the most common alternative location.

The feasibility of production relocation is low, certainly in the short term. The closure of a plant involves disengagement costs such as redundancy payments, transfer and set-up costs, and the loss of production incurred. Furthermore, where plants are linked within an overall enterprise strategy, closure can have serious repercussions for global production patterns and coordination. The significance of intra-enterprise trade, trade between the affiliates of the same enterprise, which now accounts for around one-third of total world trade, lends support to the importance of such costs. This constraint is likely to be particularly effective in the case of affiliates serving large local markets. One argument is that internationally competitive firms usually wish to remain in their preferred locations and, in fact, offer considerable stability to employees and local communities.[43]

The limited credibility of the closure threat is reinforced with recognition of the alternative strategies available to MNEs. A more feasible longer-term bargaining strategy concerns the placement of new investment elsewhere. The threat of redirection of incremental investment may emerge as a bargaining tactic of considerable effect. A second strategy relates to the use of offshore sourcing discussed in Chapter 2. Overall, the constraints on production location within MNEs suggest that this practice is not likely to present a major source of bargaining advantage. Indeed, within advanced nations, the bunching of job losses by both timing and sector, as has happened in the steel and garment industries, suggests that this phenomenon may be traced to structural changes in the world economy.

The second source of MNE management bargaining power results from the supposed limited impact of strike action on affiliates. One view is that the multiproduct nature of many MNEs means that production and revenue losses incurred on one product line in the face of a stoppage can be offset through cross-subsidization. The effect of this is to reduce management disagreement costs of union demands. Clearly, this source of advantage does not depend on multinationality; rather, it is characteristic of multiproduct firms. A more specific advantage may result from the MNEs' ability to switch production across national boundaries. The significance of production switching depends on two factors: the existence of duplicate facilities and the use of these facilities. Cases of production switching appear few and far between. Management may be curtailed in strike circumvention by opposition in related plants.

The third source of bargaining advantage refers to the expertise of management negotiators within MNEs. The transfer of experience across national boundaries may confer upon management a considerable advantage. The limited evidence that directly addresses this question does not support any management advantage. It would be rare for parent organizations to offer research support in the handling of collective bargaining issues.

Greater validity may attach to the fourth source of bargaining advantage, the insensitivity and obscurity of MNE negotiation processes which results from the centralization of decision-making. The source of these difficulties appears not so much to be the failure to decentralize decision-making authority but rather the elaborate arrangements for higher-level consultation within MNEs.

Offsetting these apparent advantages are two disadvantages of MNEs. The first is that their large size and high profile means that they will often seek to avoid conflict and the adverse publicity this may bring. The second derives from the likely interdependencies between MNE affiliates, particularly under a global strategy. Internal firm trade means that production disruption in one location can impose additional costs on other parts of an integrated production system. The idea of a bargaining advantage enjoyed by MNEs has been tested. On balance, the evidence is not consistent with the idea of an overwhelming advantage on the part of MNEs. If such an advantage existed, one would not expect to see an above-average incidence of disputes within foreign affiliates, higher than average pay levels by such firms, or their very considerable investments in procedures for containing and resolving bargaining disagreements and encouraging commitment.

CONCLUSIONS

This chapter examines the ways that globalization might influence labor relations practices. Because multinational enterprises are now the dominant business form in the global economy, their labor relations practices have a significant impact on labor markets. Research suggests that MNEs pursue labor relations practices that often differ in type or degree from those normally observed in their host country. The most distinctive features are a desire for decentralization and independence in negotiation. Globalization has coincided with a decline in union organization levels, certainly in the United States. However, this appears to be more attributable to demographic and structural change than to globalization. To increase their representation and legitimacy in the workplace, unions may need to move beyond the traditional adversarial stance to a more consensual mode, one in which they facilitate labor commitment, cooperation, and productivity improvement.

There is support for some of the concerns of organized labor. The most pressing difficulties are associated with the information disclosure practices of MNEs and their bargaining structures, which may impede labor's access to key decision makers. While threats of plant closure and resort to offshore sourcing have increased in the era of globalization, one should be sceptical of the view that MNE management enjoys an overwhelming bargaining advantage. Some indirect evidence of relative power is provided by trends in the share of national income between capital (businesses) and labor. Such analysis suggests that shares have not changed substantially in the global era. Certainly for the United States there has been remarkable stability, with wages and salaries accounting for 71.6 percent of national income in 2000. The 50-year average is 71.7 percent. Globally and regionally integrated MNEs appear vulnerable to production disruption and bargaining overtures. The high levels of disagreement costs faced by MNE management can help explain their considerable efforts to reform labor relations and to ensure labor-management accord.

Globalization and International Human Resource Management

INTRODUCTION

In this chapter, we keep our focus at the level of the international firm and examine the more general issue of developing and managing human resources. **Human resources management (HRM)** is the set of activities directed at attracting, developing, and maintaining the effective work force necessary to achieve a firm's objectives. HRM includes recruiting and selecting staff, providing training and development, appraising performance, and providing compensation and benefits.

International HRM is increasingly recognized as a major determinant of success or failure in global business. By sending managers overseas and managing their successful return home and retention, international companies can develop a management group with a

global perspective and a familiarity with the company's interests and operations in its foreign subsidiaries. This can provide
a strong competitive edge in world markets.

International HRM is considerably more complex than
human resource management within purely domestic firms.
Several factors distinguish international from domestic HRM.
First, to operate in a global business, a human resources
department must engage in a number of activities that would
not be necessary in a domestic environment. These include
international taxation issues, international relocation, and
administrative services for **expatriates** (parent-country workers).
Second, a broader perspective is necessary. Because international
human resource managers face the problem of designing and
administering programs for a variety of employee groups (such
as parent-country nationals, host-country nationals, and
third-country nationals), they need to take a more global
view of issues. Complex equity issues with regard to selection,
promotion, and pay can arise when employees of various nationalities work together, and the resolution of these issues is a major
challenge for the HRM department. Third, a greater degree of
involvement in employees' personal lives is necessary for
the selection, training, and effective management of parent-
country employees. Human resource managers may be responsible for housing, health care, taxation, and even recreational
activities of their employees. Fourth, as foreign activities become
more important, the emphasis placed on various human resource
functions changes. For example, as the need for expatriates
declines and more trained host-country nationals become available, resources previously allocated to areas of management of
parent-country employees are transferred to selecting, training,
and development of host-country employees. Fifth, the human
and financial consequences of failure in the international arena
are frequently more severe than in domestic business. For example, the premature return of an expatriate from an international
assignment is a persistent, high-cost problem for international

companies. The direct costs in salary, training costs, and travel and relocation expenses of such returnees may be as much as three times the domestic salary plus relocation expenses. Indirect costs such as loss of market share and damage to overseas customer relationships can also be considerable.

However, international businesses enjoy a number of advantages over purely national firms in attracting employees. First, their international operations give them access to a wide diversity of labor markets, with varying cost and quality of human resources. Second, multinational enterprises are able to access such markets in a variety of ways, such as directly through foreign investment and indirectly through offshore sourcing of labor-intensive tasks or accessing specialist skills through strategic alliances. For example, many multinational enterprises first entering China form joint ventures with local firms in an attempt to gain access to political relationships and knowledge of the management of distribution systems. Third, international firms enjoy advantages in the retention and development of human resources. They offer higher levels of pay and enhanced opportunities for staff development through overseas placements within their international networks of affiliates.

This chapter will focus on the human resource challenges faced by an international business. We begin by considering where to recruit staff. We then examine expatriate management and the issues that arise when staff members are assigned overseas for some time. The competitive challenges of the global era are demanding new skills and abilities in senior management. We discuss the changing nature of expatriate management and the emergence of so-called global managers. The distinctive characteristics of global managers, and how such characteristics can best be developed, are also highlighted. Finally, we look at the ways in which global competition has affected the position of women managers and whether or not they have benefited from globalization.

STAFFING POLICY

Staffing policy is concerned with the selection of employees for particular jobs. Three types of staffing policy have been identified in international business. Management staff can be chosen solely from the parent-country nationals; a mixed staff can be utilized, in which parent-country nationals occupy key positions at corporate headquarters, while host-country nationals manage subsidiaries; or the best candidate can be tapped for management staff, regardless of nationality.

Management by Parent-Country Nationals

The first staffing policy is one in which all key management positions are filled by parent-country nationals. At one time, this practice was very widespread. Firms such as Procter & Gamble, Philips, and Matsushita originally followed it (Figure 5.1). In many Japanese firms, such as Toyota and Matsushita, Japanese nationals still hold key positions in international operations.

Firms pursue this staffing policy for three reasons. First, the firm may believe there is a lack of qualified individuals in the host country to fill senior management positions. This argument is heard most frequently when the firm operates in a less-developed country. Second, the firm may see management by parent-country nationals as the best way to maintain common reporting standards and management processes across all business operations. For example, many Japanese firms prefer their foreign operations to be headed by expatriate Japanese managers because these managers have been socialized into the firm's culture while they were employed in Japan. Such a policy is favored when the firm enjoys a competitive advantage resulting from consistent approaches to labor management and quality assurance. Third, if the firm is trying to create value by transferring its domestic skills to foreign operations, it may believe that the best way to do this is to transfer overseas parent-country nationals who have those skills

Figure 5.1   Corporate giant Procter & Gamble's corporate
headquarters is located in Cincinnati, Ohio, but it conducts business
all over the world. Its traditional management style was to choose
their overseas staff solely from the United States—the parent country.
This staffing policy has declined significantly as companies have
realized the benefits of having host-country nationals in key
management positions and the difficulty that many expatriate
managers experience in adapting to a new country.

This staffing approach has declined significantly. There are
three main reasons for this. First, this staffing policy limits
advancement and development opportunities for host-country
nationals. This can lead to resentment, lower productivity, and
increased turnover among that group. Second, such an approach
can result in the firm's failure to understand host-country cultural differences that require different management styles. The
adaptation of expatriate managers can take a long time, during
which they may make costly mistakes with respect to consumer
behavior, distribution channels, and political relations. Third,
parent-country nationals are often expensive to relocate and
maintain in the host country.

Mixed Management

A second option requires host-country nationals be recruited to manage subsidiaries, while parent-country nationals occupy key positions at corporate headquarters. In many ways, this approach is a response to the shortcomings of a management team made up of only parent-country nationals. Experienced international organizations such as Shell, DuPont, and AT&T hire host-country nationals instead of transferring their domestic staff to work in professional positions in foreign operations. Host-country managers are less likely to make the mistakes arising from cultural misunderstandings that expatriate managers are prone to. A second advantage is that a mixed approach may be cheaper to implement. Host-country nationals are likely to be less expensive to maintain than expatriates.

However, this approach also has its drawbacks. Host-country nationals have limited opportunities to gain experience outside their own country and thus may not progress beyond senior positions in their own subsidiary. Again, this may cause resentment. The major weakness, however, is a gap that can form between host-country and parent-country managers. Language barriers, national loyalties, and cultural differences may isolate corporate headquarters staff from the various foreign subsidiaries. The result can be a federation of largely independent national units with only weak links to the corporate headquarters.

Multinational Management

The third option seeks the best people for key jobs throughout the organization, regardless of nationality. There are a number of advantages to this policy. First, it enables the firm to make the best use of its human resources. Second, it allows the firm to build a group of international managers who are comfortable in a number of different cultures. The creation of such a group may be a critical first step toward building a strong unifying corporate culture and an informal management network, both of which are required for a global business strategy. In addition, the multinational composition of the management team tends to reduce cultural misunderstandings and to enhance responsiveness to local market conditions.

However, there are a number of difficulties in pursuing a multinational staffing policy. Many countries want foreign subsidiaries to employ their local citizens. They use immigration laws to require the employment of host-country nationals possessing the necessary skills. Most host countries require firms to provide extensive documentation if they wish to hire a foreign national instead of a local national. A further problem is that this staffing policy can be very expensive to implement. There are increased training costs, relocation costs involved in transferring managers from country to country, and the need for a compensation structure with a standardized international base pay level that may be higher than national levels in many countries.

The choice of staffing policy is affected by national culture. European companies are more likely than U.S. or Japanese firms to choose managers regardless of nationality. This approach is encouraged in the European Union by firms wishing to improve the mobility of workers and managers throughout Europe. Japanese firms favor their own nationals, in part because employing Japanese managers in key roles in foreign subsidiaries facilitates the control of key business processes such as engineering and quality control. However, Japanese firms sometimes rely too heavily on this model, to their own disadvantage. While they usually hire host-country nationals for lower-level positions, they are reluctant to use non-Japanese managers in higher-level positions. Further, non-Japanese managers often face a "glass ceiling" because the top positions in the firm are reserved for Japanese nationals. Therefore, the best host-country managers will seek more challenge and responsibility by leaving to work for non-Japanese employers.

MANAGEMENT OF EXPATRIATES

Regardless of the choice of staffing policy, almost all international businesses need to place staff overseas for various reasons. This may be because of a shortage of managers locally, to enhance the skills and experience of a particular individual, or to build global capability within the firm. In deciding the best-qualified candidates for overseas assignments, companies have to realize that expatriates in a foreign country are faced with circumstances that can be very different from those of their home country. With an overseas assignment, managers are not only changing jobs but also changing their way of life. As a result, companies need suitable selection processes for candidates and their family members when contemplating sending them on an overseas assignment.

Despite this need, there do not seem to be valid and reliable screening devices to identify managers who are likely to succeed in a foreign assignment. However, a number of appropriate criteria are easily identifiable. First, the adaptability and flexibility of candidates and their spouse or family to new environments should be important factors in selection. Most expatriate failure is not caused by inadequate technical skills but by the inability of expatriates and their families to adjust to an unfamiliar culture. Thus, expatriates should have the ability to adapt to new circumstances and situations and to respond flexibly to different ideas. Moreover, they should have the ability to solve problems within different frameworks, including culture, politics, religion and ethics, and from different perspectives.

Second, technical competence in a job is very important when expatriates are located some distance from headquarters, or the center of technical expertise, and cannot consult as readily with their peers and superiors at headquarters on matters related to their job. However, a manager's effectiveness overseas depends on more than just technical skills. In many situations "people skills" and cross-cultural sensitivity may be more important than technical skills.

Third, personality traits and the ability of expatriates to deal effectively with their superiors, peers, subordinates, business associates, and clients are an important determinant of successful performance. This includes the ability to relate to, live with, and work among people whose value systems, beliefs, customs, manners, and ways of conducting business may differ greatly from one's own. Hence, a candidate should be a person who has cultural empathy, which is an understanding, open-mindedness, awareness of, and willingness to probe for the reasons people of another culture behave the way they do.

Fourth, expatriates should be able to transmit information and communicate well because they serve as an interface between the home office and locals, and sometimes the host government. Therefore, the expatriate manager should be a skilled negotiator. Expatriates sometimes have to train local replacements and transfer knowledge to their local colleagues; therefore, they should also have teaching skills.

Fifth, a candidate's knowledge of a host country's language and the willingness to use a foreign language seem to be important criteria, because confidence in interacting with locals will lead to successful overseas assignments. For example, in China, knowing how to communicate in basic Chinese conversation would impress Chinese partners and help the expatriate manager to enjoy a better working and living relationship with locals.

Sixth, decision-making ability is a very important variable, especially when expatriates are operating under conditions of isolation or physical distance from the center of decision-making in the home office.

The need to give at least equal consideration to cross-cultural skills as well as technical skills has resulted in a number of approaches that international companies can use. The Korean electronics conglomerate LG formally assesses all employees through a questionnaire survey. Any identified weaknesses are addressed through appropriate training, and personalized development plans and timetables for improvement are drawn up. This ensures that the company has an extensive management pool upon which to draw. In contrast, Colgate-Palmolive recruits students from universities who can demonstrate considerable international orientation through travel, language acquisition, or cross-cultural experience. These employees are given relatively short overseas trial training assignments and are then evaluated in the light of these assignments.

Expatriate Failure

Two of the three staffing strategies outlined above rely on extensive use of expatriates. In one, the expatriates are all parent-country nationals who are transferred abroad. In the other, the multinational management approach, the expatriates need not be parent-country nationals. Despite the most careful selection and training programs some expatriates are going to fail.

Expatriate failure may be defined as either employees who return to the home country prematurely or expatriates who are unable to achieve business objectives or perform effectively in a foreign country. If expatriates fail to thrive, companies are likely to face significant direct and indirect costs.

A decade of research involving expatriates from more than 750 companies suggests that between 10 and 20 percent of all U.S. managers sent overseas returned early because of difficulties, while nearly one-third of those who stayed the full duration of the assignment did not perform as expected.[44] Furthermore, within a year of repatriation, one-quarter had left their company, often to work for a competitor. That rate was twice that of managers who have not been sent on overseas assignments. This suggests that where an expatriation assignment increases the capabilities of the individual manager, this must be recognized and rewarded upon repatriation. Many companies appear to expect the expatriate to return and simply resume previous responsibilities. The resulting frustration may encourage early resignation.

However, these costs are not as serious as the indirect costs. Indirect costs include the loss of time and business opportunities; damaged relations with the host country government, with local organizations and with direct customers in the foreign country; and even a long-term negative impact upon the firm's reputation in the region. For expatriates themselves, costs can include damaged career prospects, emotional upheaval, reduced self-esteem and self-confidence, lack of job satisfaction, lost prestige among peers, and diminished motivation.

Many factors contribute to expatriate failure. One is poor selection. Some companies select staff to send abroad hurriedly due to the need to resolve a staffing crisis in an overseas subsidiary. Sometimes the selection process overemphasizes technical skills at the expense of such factors as the expatriate's personality, ability, emotional characteristics, family situation, and knowledge of the host country's culture. Failure may be due to a lack of preparation for expatriates and their families. Pre-departure preparation should include critical family issues such as the role of the partner, children's schools, medical coverage, and making friends. Failure may also occur because of inadequate support mechanisms including compensation packages and career support.

THE CHANGING NATURE OF EXPATRIATE MANAGEMENT

Today, traditional expatriate policies are being reconsidered. On the one hand, the high costs of expatriate failure have encouraged international human resource managers to give careful consideration to their expatriate policies. On the other hand, and equally important, are changes in the business environment such as globalization, strategic alliances, and regional strategies, which are rendering the traditional expatriate model increasingly ineffective. A number of forces are bringing opportunities or pressures for major change in staffing strategy and policy. The global spread of education is providing more people with higher-level skills worldwide. This makes it easier to find managers locally. In addition, the constant development of global tele-communications has provided better access to resources, wider coverage, and lower costs of managing an international business. Better telecommunications have helped to break down international barriers and have made it feasible to manage operations from a distance, thereby reducing the need to bring in outside management. Many governments want international firms to optimize and utilize the talent pool available domestically.

The Expatriate Manager versus the Global Manager

The rapid globalization of business requires a new breed of international executive, the global manager. Success in global business depends on the effective development of such managers. One influential study defined a global manager as "an executive assigned to a position with a cross-border responsibility, who has a flexible and open mind, with a well-rounded understanding of international business and ability to work across cultural and functional boundaries, who perceives global competition as an opportunity, and who is able to balance the simultaneous demands of global integration and national responsiveness."[45] The key contrasts between expatriate and global managers are summarized in Table 5.1.

The characteristics required of a global manager are more likely to be found within third-country nationals (TCNs) than parent-country nationals (PCNs), and this is encouraging a shift in staffing strategies to favor the former. TCNs are frequently multilingual, that is, they have the ability to work in more than one language, and may exhibit greater cultural sensitivity due to their multicultural experiences. Also, a TCN manager is often assigned to a host country based on earlier demonstrated skills and performance, generally the result of positions held in a number of different countries, compared to the PCN who traditionally has been selected on the basis of technical ability with little attention paid to international experience. Moreover, international companies have found that TCNs tend to cost less

Table 5.1   Contrasts Between Expatriate and Global Managers

	EXPATRIATE MANAGER	GLOBAL MANAGER
Global perspective	Focuses on a single foreign country and on managing relationships between headquarters and that country	Understands the worldwide business environment from a global perspective
Local responsiveness	Becomes an expert on one culture	Must learn about many foreign cultures, perspectives, tastes, trends, and approaches to conducting business
Synergistic learning	Works with and coaches people in each foreign culture separately or sequentially Integrates foreigners into the headquarters' national organizational culture	Works within and learns from people from many cultures simultaneously Creates a culturally synergistic organizational environment
Transition and adaptation	Adapts to living in a foreign culture	Adapts to living in many foreign cultures
Cross-culture interaction	Uses cross-cultural interaction skills primarily on foreign assignments	Uses cross-cultural skills on a daily basis throughout career
Collaboration	Interacts with colleagues from within clearly defined hierarchies of structural and cultural dominance and subordination	Interacts with foreign colleagues as equals
Foreign experience	Expatriation or inpatriation primarily to get the job done	Transpatriation for career and organizational development

Source: Adler, N.J. and S. Bartholomew. "Managing Globally Competent People." *Academy of Management Executive* vol. 6, no. 3 (1992): 52–65.

in terms of salary and other benefits. They are also less likely to experience conflict between loyalty to the organization and loyalty to the host country.

However, host governments that place importance on local hiring may consider TCNs just as unacceptable as PCNs. Despite such concerns, international businesses are sending capable people from all parts of the world to a wide variety of locations to develop their global and cross-cultural skills. In this way, such firms develop a group of globally sophisticated managers. Foreign appointments are no longer used simply to get a job done in a foreign country, but increasingly are used to enhance organizational and individual learning in all parts of the system.

These tendencies are being reinforced by the trend towards greater teamwork, particularly cross-functional teams that comprise different cultures, languages, locations, and time zones. While work teams have long been established at the national level, they are now being created at the international level. The principal source of such skills is internal, and this has created a new staffing strategy, that of inpatriation.

Inpatriation involves the transfer of international managers from their overseas assignments to the home market on a permanent or semipermanent basis. Inpatriation provides a significant source of international management skills and allows the creation of truly multicultural and multinational organizations. It also offers a speedy alternative to building such organizations through the traditional process of expatriate and repatriated staff. An excellent example is provided by Shell, which has 38 nationalities represented at its London headquarters. Inpatriate employees are also a highly effective link between the parent and subsidiary businesses, assisting in the attainment of both cultural and strategic consistency.

Research suggests that successful global managers share a core set of characteristics, including inquisitiveness, perspective, character, and savvy. [46] Inquisitiveness is the driving factor and is characteristic of global leaders who thrive on learning opportunities that result from the diversity of the international business environment. Perspective describes an attitude of acceptance of uncertainty and an ability to balance the tensions

Sir Richard Branson—Successful Global Manager

Sir Richard Branson started business life as a hippy entrepreneur with a flair for publicity. Born in England in 1950 and educated at Stowe School, he went into business at 16, publishing "Student" magazine. By the age of 20, he was the subject of a television documentary.

Having originally founded Virgin as a mail-order record company, he later opened his first store in London's Oxford Street. The Virgin Records music label was formed in 1972. [. . .] When punk came along, Virgin signed the outrageous Sex Pistols when other record companies refused to touch them. The move turned out to be a marketing coup. Many other stars were signed up, including Genesis, Peter Gabriel, Simple Minds, and The Rolling Stones, making Virgin Records a major player in the international music business.

Since then Virgin has expanded into air and rail travel, mobile phones, finance, retail, internet, drinks, hotels and leisure, with around 200 companies in over 30 countries. [. . .]

In the mid-1980s the Branson company was floated on the Stock Exchange, but the Branson style didn't fit the way City [of London] institutions expected public companies to behave. So he bought the company back from the shareholders. To find the money he had to sell Virgin Records to Thorn-EMI. Even so, the price, agreed in 1992, was huge, at almost £500 million.

In 2000 Virgin launched a series of new businesses including Virgin Cars, Virgin Wines, Virgin Student, *Virgin Money.com*, Virgin Energy, and *Virgin Travelstore.com*. [. . .]

Then, the final frontier. In September 2004, Sir Richard signed a £14m contract to have five "spaceliners" built in the U.S., set to take Virgin passengers into space by around 2008.

Source: "Profile: Richard Branson." BBC News World Service. Available online at *http://news.bbc.co.uk/1/hi/uk/3693588.stm.*

between global integration and the need for local adaptation. Character is manifested through exceptional interpersonal skills and the ability to demonstrate a high level of integrity in a variety of ambiguous situations. Savvy is the ability to identify

Richard Branson's latest adventure will take Virgin passengers into space. In September 2004, Branson signed a contract to have five "spaceliners" built in the United States, scheduled to take Virgin passengers into space by around 2008.

and exploit global business opportunities. It requires excellent perceptual and organizational skills.

These characteristics can be developed in a number of ways. According to global executives interviewed, they acquired these characteristics through travel, teamwork, training, and transfers. With overseas travel, the intensity of travel is critical. Simply going overseas is not enough; it is the quality of interactions that create learning experiences. Working in global teams provides opportunities for prolonged interaction with a wide diversity of individuals. Again, this gives exposure to a range of different values and business models. Training offers a structured process for the assimilation of conceptual skills that provide a framework for the interpretation of experience. Executives believe that transfers offer the most powerful development experiences and reflect the traditional role of expatriate assignments. These findings highlight the increasingly general nature of desirable characteristics of future global leaders who will face a challenging array of complex problems stemming from a dynamically shifting business environment and competitive landscape.

WOMEN MANAGERS IN THE GLOBAL ECONOMY

There is limited understanding of how the economic well being of women has been affected by globalization. Several difficulties arise when examining this issue. First, women are not a homogeneous category. The effects of globalization vary according to geographical location, education, and skill levels, as well as access to productive resources. Second, globalization is not developing in a uniform way; its impact on women in the advanced economies is likely to be quite different from the effects experienced in the poorest parts of the world. Similarly, unpredictable events such as the terrorist attacks of September 11, 2001, can dramatically shift the path of globalization. The majority of Afghan women have seen their freedom and well being increase significantly since the U.S. attack on Afghanistan that began in 2001 (Figure 5.2). Third, the culture and internal preparedness

Figure 5.2   Businesswomen from Afghanistan listen to a professor of management at Thunderbird, the Gavin School of International Management in Glendale, Arizona, in January 2005. These women hope to learn business skills that will help them form their own businesses in their home country.

of a country will influence the impact of globalization. If women have equal access to education and training, and enjoy social and political freedom, they are better placed to respond positively to the opportunities offered by globalization. Similarly, the level of modernization, industrialization, and technological capability of a country will moderate its experience with globalization. Fourth, it is difficult to assess the impact of globalization on women's welfare in part because of deficiencies in the measurement of women's economic contribution. Much of the work done by women goes unreported or is seriously underreported. The United Nations estimates that the monetary value of the world economy represents only 59 percent of real global output and that more than two-thirds of the difference is accounted for by women's unpaid work.

The impacts of globalization on the economic position of women are both positive and negative. On the one hand, globalization brings new employment opportunities to developing countries; indeed much of the growth in developing countries has been the result of female employment. The spread of information and communications technology can improve employment flexibility for women. Where globalization brings modernization, constraints on women resulting from tradition may be eased. On the other hand, many of the jobs created are low paid, unstable, and hazardous. The competitive pressures accompanying globalization can encourage excessive work hours and deterioration in working conditions. Whether, on balance, women benefit from globalization or not, is not clear.

In this section we will focus on the likely effects of globalization on women managers. Women are significantly underrepresented in the ranks of management. While women constitute 46 percent of the American work force, they account for only 3 percent of senior executives and less than half of 1 percent of the highest-paid managers and directors.[47] While these figures are extremely low, they represent considerable progress in recent years. Women managers have benefited from favorable economic and demographic conditions, greater social acceptance of women's careers, and supportive government policies. The expansion of service industries—including banking and other financial services, as well as public services—has increased demand for women managers. Economic growth and intense competition have added to the demand for top-quality managers regardless of gender.

Despite these favorable conditions, women managers still face considerable barriers. As well as general problems of discrimination, women suffer from traditional attitudes towards their domestic and family roles; their limited access to the networks developed in schools, universities, and the military that men enjoy; and widely held stereotypical views of women's qualifications and abilities. While many more women have obtained managerial positions, these have been at lower levels. Progress up the managerial ranks appears to be extremely difficult.

A number of explanations for this situation have been proposed. The earliest explanations emphasized personality and behavioral differences between men and women. They suggested that if male characteristics were associated with managerial success, the limited progress of women could be explained in terms of their differences. Such a view suffers a number of shortcomings. First, researchers found few significant differences between the genders when similar jobs were studied. Second, the acknowledged strengths of women in mentoring and relationship building are the very traits that international organizations seek to cultivate in the global economy.

Later explanations incorporated the role of organizational context, highlighting the power, prestige, and rewards enjoyed by men as determinants of organizational attitudes and behavior. In this way, the lower-level positions held by women were seen as simply confirming their lack of ambition. In addition, some authors have argued that behavior within organizations is not gender-neutral and discrimination may be prompted by men's desire to limit the competition they face for top-level positions.

Each of these perspectives suggests different policy responses. The first perspective, one based on individual differences, implies that women managers need to change, to become more like successful male managers. Organizational context and power explanations create quite different policy prescriptions, suggesting that the responsibility for change lies with employers and the most senior company executives. Perhaps the most effective force for change is the continuing shortage of top-quality managers. As global operations and competition become more demanding, companies are forced to rethink their discriminatory stereotypes and to attract the best management talent, regardless of gender.

CONCLUSIONS

This chapter has considered the challenges of international human resource management within a global business. International human resource management is an important and demanding function within global businesses because people and their skills underpin the competitiveness of these firms.

Decisions with regard to staffing policy involve choices about the mix of parent-country, host-country, and third-country nationals within the firm. Each strategic choice offers both strengths and weaknesses. Regardless of the particular mix, many managers are assigned overseas as expatriates. However, the traditional practice of expatriate management is not sufficient in the global era. Increasingly, international businesses seek truly global managers, those who embrace the challenges, tensions, and learning opportunities characteristic of international business. The global shortage of such individuals means that companies are increasing their workplace diversity to the advantage of women managers. While there are now more women managers than ever, they remain bunched within lower-level management positions.

This discussion provides a number of conclusions. The first is the centrality of the human resource management function within the international business. This was not always the case. In many international businesses power was predominately concentrated within the finance, marketing, or engineering functions. HRM was seen simply as a service function. This is no longer true. Increasingly, a firm's human resources are its key resource and, as such, must be managed appropriately and effectively.

Second, globalization has brought both qualitative and quantitative changes in the nature of competition. As businesses find it increasingly difficult to compete on the basis of cost, quality, or even technology, they have sought to develop new sustainable sources of competitive advantage including creativity, customer service, branding, and continuous learning. All of these behavioral sources of advantage are embedded within the organization's human resources.

Third, globalization is increasing workplace diversity and forcing firms to develop new approaches to management and to revise long-held stereotypical positions. Women managers have benefited from these changes but still find themselves disadvantaged at the most senior levels. However, global competition and a worldwide shortage of highly skilled managers may provide the best environment for improving the position of women managers.

Fourth, globalization is dramatically altering management styles and approaches. International businesses are only now beginning to understand the sorts of characteristics and experiences that will be critical for tomorrow's leaders. Finding and developing such people is undoubtedly the major challenge facing the international human resource management function.

Policy Responses

INTRODUCTION

We have seen that globalization has brought significant changes to the nature of global labor markets and the challenges that workers face. Critics of globalization argue that contemporary capitalism is characterized by the so-called three "I"s—instability, insecurity, and inequality. Furthermore, they see globalization as a process that has radically changed the power of capital and labor. Companies enjoy considerable freedom to move capital, technology, and production across national borders, while the mobility of labor, particularly the least skilled, is limited. Markets that have been opened up to global competition—capital and goods markets—are characterized by high levels of insecurity.

In the light of such impacts, there is considerable interest in designing appropriate policies to correct or improve the workings of labor markets. However, the design and implementation of such policies is both complex and controversial. Policies are difficult to design, because while it is generally agreed that significant changes have occurred, it is not clear to what extent these changes are the result of globalization rather than the result of other factors, such as technological change. This ambiguity is most apparent in the areas of employment and earnings. Controversy surrounds the likely effectiveness of policies in this area and their differing impacts. Acting to assist displaced workers in the advanced economies may come at the expense of jobs, incomes, and growth in developing countries. In the same way, policies that enhance returns on education and skill may be of little benefit to the least skilled.

Different perceptions of the impact of globalization on labor generate contrasting policy recommendations. In Table 6.1, we identify three key perspectives operating at two levels: the national and the international. Those who see labor at a disadvantage as a result of globalization argue for intervention limiting the power of capital (business) or increasing the power of labor in an attempt to redress the balance of power. Their worldview focuses on the struggle between capital and labor for shares of the national product, irrespective of the size of that product. Relative shares depend on the balance of bargaining power.

Trade economists take a different perspective. They advocate the maximization of global output and see the distribution of that product reflecting scarcity and productivity, not bargaining power. They are more likely to favor market-based policies that attempt to improve the position of labor through increased consumer choice (the option to buy socially or ethically assured products or services). Labor advocates support direct intervention as an effective way of increasing labor's share. From the trade perspective, the same policies reduce output and alter relative shares only by changing the nature of the markets that determine factor returns. In this chapter we examine these options, evaluating their usefulness and likely impacts on labor.

Table 6.1　Policy Options

EFFECT ON BARGAINING POWER	LIMITING THE POWER OF CAPITAL	INCREASING THE POWER OF LABOR	MARKET-BASED POLICIES
National	Host or source nation regulation of trade/foreign direct investment/ offshore sourcing Bilateral trade/ investment agreements	Employee partici-pation in decision making	Growth and national development Labor market adjustment programs
International	Information disclosure and collection	Labor standards Codes of conduct Multinational labor cooperation and bargaining	Social labeling Voluntary codes of conduct Ethical trading arrangements Facilitating eco-nomic growth and development Restructuring global processes

POLICIES TO LIMIT THE POWER OF BUSINESS

The first set of policies is designed to limit the power of busi-ness, particularly multinational enterprises operating across national borders. Initiatives at the national level focus on host-country or parent-nation regulation of trade, investment, and offshore sourcing. A nation hosting foreign investment could require that investing firms commit themselves to specific labor standards or to respect local labor relations practices. Similarly, a source nation may require its firms to abide by standards in its overseas operations comparable to those practiced at home. Restrictions within the United States on the offshore sourcing

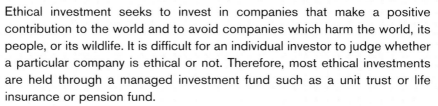

What Is Ethical Investment?

Ethical investment seeks to invest in companies that make a positive contribution to the world and to avoid companies which harm the world, its people, or its wildlife. It is difficult for an individual investor to judge whether a particular company is ethical or not. Therefore, most ethical investments are held through a managed investment fund such as a unit trust or life insurance or pension fund.

There are funds that merely exclude investment in specific activities or industries such as tobacco, gambling, alcohol, and armaments. Others take a more proactive stance, actively looking to invest in companies involved in environmentally sound, socially progressive businesses. [. . .]

The roots of modern ethical investment may be traced to the 1920s. The Methodist Church in North America decided to invest in the stock market, having previously viewed it as a form of gambling. However, they wished to exclude certain types of companies, specifically those involved in alcohol or gambling. The Quakers soon followed, but they were especially keen to avoid weapons manufacture.

Public demand for ethical investment vehicles took off in America with the launch of the Pax Fund in 1971 as a reaction against the Vietnam War. Discontent caused by the Vietnam War had led some investors to question how their money was being used. [. . .]

There are two main reasons why you would consider investing in ethical investment funds. First, you may feel it appropriate that your investment decisions should mirror your own personal views and behavior. Ethical investment helps you to invest according to your principles.

Second, by investing ethically you can gently influence companies to improve their ethical record. If companies found that unethical behavior caused investors to withdraw their money, it would make them think twice.

Source: Moneyextra Guides. Available online at *http://www.moneyworld.co.uk/faqs/ethfaq3.htm.*

of federal government work are an example of action by one source nation.

Host-nation regulation may discourage current and future investments. The problem is particularly acute for nations forming part of a regional economic group like the European Union (EU) or where investors see a high degree of substitutability between different locations. For instance, software engineering work can be outsourced to India, Eastern Europe, and, increasingly, China. Unilateral policy initiatives of this form invariably disadvantage the implementing nation, where potential investors see such requirements as unnecessary or burdensome.

Source-nation regulation of global business activities, while eliminating the problem of host- nation competition and substitution, is also subject to a fundamental limitation. Such control, when implemented in isolation, means that regulated international businesses are likely to suffer a competitive disadvantage if regulation raises costs or limits freedom of action. In industries subject to high levels of global competition, such as electronics or soft drinks, unregulated competitors are likely to gain market share. There are two probable business responses to such regulation, both of which lower the likelihood or effectiveness of such policies. Some firms will formally incorporate themselves (or certain business activities) in unregulated locations—a situation long established in the world shipping industry, where a considerable percentage of the world fleet is registered in countries such as Panama and Liberia. Alternatively, intense business lobbying will see such proposals either abandoned or sufficiently diluted to be of only limited effectiveness.

An alternative to unilateral regulation is the development of bilateral agreements between two nations. For example, the recent U.S.-Singapore trade agreement contained a section on labor standards. A precedent for such agreements can be found in the more than 2,000 bilateral investment treaties currently in existence. However, bilateral agreements are themselves subject to a number of shortcomings. If dual nation labor regulation raises operating costs, trade, investment, or work can be diverted into non-participating countries.

The limitations of unilateral and bilateral action in labor and social regulation have favored the search for international initiatives. The problem of obtaining meaningful and current information on the operations of international businesses has led to the inclusion of information-disclosure provisions in most codes of conduct. However, the significance of this problem, from the perspective of both union negotiators and host governments, has created pressure for two supplementary provisions. One provision is a mandatory directive providing employee information and consultation rights. The second provision is the establishment of an international agency charged with the collection, analysis, and dissemination of information on the operations of international firms. The first strategy has been pursued most effectively within the EU and will be considered in the section below. The task of collecting and analyzing information has increasingly been assumed by a range of **non-governmental organizations** (**NGOs**) that have publicized the labor practices of international firms.

POLICIES TO INCREASE THE POWER OF LABOR

An alternative approach to securing labor rights is to focus on increasing labor's relative power. We can again distinguish between national and international initiatives. At the national level, proposals are concerned with increasing labor's access to corporate decision-making processes. One view is that the strongest hope for organized labor in countering the power of international firms lies in access to senior management and board of directors-level decision-making. One option is host-country councils that enable worker representatives to participate in the decision-making processes of particular firms. A variant of this is company councils that help bring together union representatives of the same business from a number of countries.

Employee Participation in Decision Making

Increased employee participation in enterprise decision making has long been a concern in the EU's industrial relations policy. While the ultimate objective seems to be to place employees on companies' board of directors, in the shorter term, the diversity of national business systems has led to acceptance of a variety of arrangements among member nations. This diversity reflects the likelihood of slow progress towards convergence of employee representation even within a relatively homogeneous group like the European Union.

Many advocates of enhanced labor power within the global economy believe that international initiatives are likely to be more effective. While some aspire to multinational union cooperation and bargaining as the ultimate response, the limited progress of such strategies means that more pragmatic options have been developed. These include the linking of trade and labor standards, and the adoption of codes of conduct.

Global Trade and Labor Standards

Proposals for linking labor standards to trade are controversial. The strongest advocates, such as the AFL-CIO, want to see enforceable labor rights embedded within U.S. trade agreements and within the **World Trade Organization (WTO)**. Where trading partners fail to uphold specific labor standards, they would be punished through trade sanctions. Developing countries have tended to oppose such proposals, in part because they fear an erosion of their competitive advantage in labor-intensive production. Furthermore, such standards would protect competing workers in the developed countries as well as providing a means to allow these countries to deny market access to offending countries.

It is useful to draw a distinction between core (or basic), and developmental (or economic) labor standards. Core labor standards cover specific legal rights such as the right to form unions or prohibit undesirable practices such as forced or child labor.[48]

These standards are generally believed to provide the minimum necessary conditions for the efficient operation of a modern labor market. However, economic welfare is not likely to be maximized when countries adopt universal standards. Core standards eliminate some of the differences in comparative advantage that make trade attractive, reducing the potential gains from trade. Because of the differing levels of development and areas of market failure, each country should seek solutions to its problems of market failure. There is no obvious case for the adoption of core standards.

Developmental labor standards are those likely to vary according to the development level of an economy and typically include standards for the minimum wage and overtime rates. These are the standards that if imposed from outside could limit the competitiveness of developing economies. For example, a global minimum wage needs to take into account varying levels of productivity, since wages are expected to reflect productivity.

Advocates of trade-related labor standards argue that globalization and increased trade, in the absence of labor standards, encourages a "race to the bottom" as competition brings a worldwide deterioration of labor conditions. This occurs as low labor standards in developing countries generate artificially low wage levels. Multinational enterprises producing labor-intensive products may be attracted to these locations. The resulting competitive pressure encourages countries with high labor standards to either face the loss of jobs, lower their standards to maintain competitiveness, or commit considerable resources to sustain higher standards. There is little compelling evidence to support this argument. Indeed, the evidence suggests that countries liberalizing their trade and investment regimes do not usually couple this with a reduction in labor standards.[49] Similarly, foreign investors are not strongly attracted to low labor standards; rather they bring higher wages and enhanced working conditions to workers in a number of developing countries, including China.[50] Low wages in developing countries reflect low productivity and are generally not the result of a government ploy to compete unfairly. In fact, there is more likely to be a positive relationship between trade and labor standards, mediated by rising income. In general, higher income countries also have higher labor standards.

Critics of trade-related labor standards believe that labor standards cannot be simply imposed from outside. In essence, trade and labor standards are part of the more general development question. Since trade is a powerful force in development, and development brings higher income levels and thus labor standards, the focus should be on ensuring development. Attempts to limit trade, or to punish countries through trade sanctions, appear misplaced.

Critics also believe that trade sanctions are neither an efficient nor a costless policy response. They are not efficient because they are a very blunt instrument.[51] In 1993, the threat of U.S sanctions against the Bangladesh garment industry led to the dismissal of all children workers below age 16. Anecdotal evidence suggests that many of these children were made worse off ending up in workshops and factories not producing for export, or as prostitutes and street vendors. Clearly, trade sanctions only affect export industries and may have little or no impact on the rest of the economy, including the informal sector, where many of the worst abuses occur. Considerable reform of WTO rules would also be required if trade sanctions are be implemented. While the WTO can support or decline sanctions imposed by individual countries, it has no mandate to impose collective or multilateral sanctions. The impact of poor labor standards must be measurable, as this would be the key determinant of the likely form, size, and duration of intended sanctions.

Trade sanctions are not costless. They restrict growth and development in the target country, reducing the likelihood of higher labor standards. They raise prices and restrict choice for consumers in the country imposing the sanctions. Sanctions also induce protectionist behavior by interest groups in the imposing country. Opportunities to use such sanctions to reduce foreign competition and raise profit levels may be pursued by interest and lobby groups. All of these costs need to be weighed against the expected benefits of the policy.

Those who believe the inefficiencies of sanctions outweigh the benefits offer more modest alternative proposals. These include reforming the International Labour Office (ILO), in particular, publishing more information and a scorecard of how well individual countries conform to core labor standards, as well as strengthening enforcement powers; developing closer links between the ILO and the WTO making clear the connection between trade and labor; and rewarding positive behavior by offering increased market access to countries maintaining high labor standards.

Codes of Conduct

Codes of conduct setting out expectations of the behavior of international firms have been enacted within a number of international bodies, the most important of which are the ILO and the **Organization for Economic Cooperation and Development (OECD)**. The codes of these organizations are important because they cover the major source nations and host nations of international business and because they are evolutionary, providing for regular review and amendment in the light of changing business practices. Codes of conduct do offer an effective and efficient method of regulating international business. Their major impact is likely to be outside the narrow area of labor relations, where research suggests that many firms believe that their labor relations practices exceed the minimum expectations set out by these codes. However, in a number of cases, code requirements have been used to clarify the obligations of multinational enterprises (MNEs) to organized labor.

Multinational Labor Cooperation and Bargaining

Many labor advocates hold the view that the most effective response to global business is some form of international union action. Several forms of such action are possible. The simplest is the collection and exchange of information on the activities of MNEs. A second stage might be one of consultation between national unions. Demonstrations of solidarity in the form of sympathy strikes, the banning of overtime, or production transfers constitute a third stage. Further cooperation might involve the coordination of demands between subsidiaries of the same company. The most complete form would be true multinational collective bargaining based on a common claim and simultaneous termination of agreements. Industries such as shipping and entertainment have come closest to experiencing true multinational labor cooperation and bargaining.

The reality is that transnational union action has been limited in both its form and effectiveness. Specialist NGOs and bodies such as the ILO have largely taken over the function of information collection. Globalization has fractured the interests of labor in developed and developing countries, and in many countries union leaders have suffered a serious decline in terms of power and influence over the past three decades.

The barriers to cooperation facing organized labor are considerable. The structure of the international labor movement is not conducive to cohesive action. Fragmentation of labor markets has led to the strong employment growth in the informal sector, an area where traditional unions have been slow to organize workers and where the initiative has passed to grassroots organizations. Labor responses to international firms have long been reactive and defensive. Furthermore, union cooperation is not likely to be effective in countering new challenges such as offshore sourcing. In previous periods of strong competition and the need for corporate restructuring, such as the 1980s, the interests of labor and business were seen as far more closely linked than they are today. The present period is one of strong business performance, with much of the adjustment cost, such as job loss, multi-skilling, and retraining, being carried by labor. Unions find it very difficult to manage the tensions between retaining their traditional ideological links, protecting worker interests in the workplace, and playing a part in the successful attraction and retention of investment. One consequence of globalization is that union organizations in different countries are more likely to view one another in competitive rather than cooperative terms. Where production involves extensive out-sourcing, the ultimate employer may be difficult to identify and confront. For all these reasons, transnational collective bargaining is rare. A more realistic way for organized labor to move forward may be to cooperate internationally to lobby for changes to the current terms of globalization.

MARKET-BASED POLICIES

The possible distortions resulting from interventionist policies and controls and the limited effectiveness of organized labor have created growing interest in market-based policy responses. Market-based policies rely on market processes and signals such as information, prices, and labeling to affect economic behavior.

At the national level, the most effective policies for strength-ening the position of labor are those that encourage growth and national development and labor market adjustment. The level of development of a country is perhaps the prime determinant of its labor standards. This suggests that policies, such as liberal-ization, openness, and deregulation, that encourage development may have the secondary effect of improving the condition of labor within that country. The irony of this should be clear. Since there are no recorded cases of economies that have enjoyed rapid growth and rising income levels by pursuing a policy of complete economic self-reliance, globalization, while seemingly creating problems for labor, also holds the key to improving labor market conditions. The simplest policy prescription, then, is more globalization. However, this view overemphasizes the efficiency benefits of globalization at the expense of equity considerations. This means that any move towards greater engagement with the world economy may need to be accompanied by supportive internal policies on industrial restructuring, social welfare, and labor market adjustment.

Labor Market Adjustment

For developed economies, globalization and the futility of protectionism increase the need for efficient internal adjustment. Generally, as less skilled jobs are lost or such work is outsourced overseas, the maintenance of employment levels requires economic upgrading and efficient labor market functioning. The ILO estimates that the OECD countries have around 40 million unemployed workers; worldwide, the figure is in excess of 800 million. The developed countries must develop knowledge, R&D (research and development) spending, and innovation, to facilitate their shift into high-technology, high-value-added products and services if they are to maintain and improve living standards. Similarly, if new technological opportunities are to be exploited, product markets should also be competitive. Adjustment policies such as the Trade Adjustment Assistance program which provides assistance to individuals who become unemployed as a result of increased imports from, or shifts in production to, foreign countries, need to be extended beyond manufacturing to include service industries.

Adjustment has its costs. One study, which focused on five U.S. import-competing industries, reported that almost two-thirds of workers who lost their jobs between 1979 and 1999 as a result of import competition eventually found new ones.[51] However, on average they experienced wage cuts of 13 percent. While one-third of those displaced maintained or improved their earnings, a quarter suffered a pay cut of at least 30 percent. Those suffering the most significant cuts were older, less-educated and less-skilled workers who had benefited from having tenure in their previous work. Labor adjustment policies are increasingly shifting from passive forms of income compensation to more active measures that assist with job searching, relocation, and retraining.

Within global economies, issues of equity are best addressed through taxation and government spending. Government spending provides education, training, and welfare nets for those in urgent need, while modest taxation levels reduce income inequality without destroying work incentives. Tax policy can also be used to influence the nature of global business activity. While there is growing concern with the practice of offshore sourcing, it is currently treated benignly in tax terms. There is scope for tax policy changes that could be used to make this option less attractive to businesses.

Voluntary Codes of Conduct

A variety of schemes that offer a more market-based approach to the creation of socially responsible brands have been proposed. One advantage of the schemes is that consumers who value socially and morally acceptable behavior purchase goods, while compensating producers for the higher costs incurred. The most important schemes include corporate codes of conduct and social labeling. Both seek to use informed consumer demand to encourage the adoption of higher labor standards.

Codes of conduct developed within multinational enterprises, as opposed to those mandated by international bodies, are designed to ensure global compliance with a predetermined set of principles, including labor practices. Since Levi Strauss & Co. adopted a code laying out criteria for the selection of trading partners in 1992, many other firms in the clothing and footwear industries have followed this lead. These codes normally outlaw forced labor, child labor, and physical and mental abuse of workers as well as encouraging respect for fundamental human rights, proper health and safety standards, and the right to organize in unions. Examples are the Clean Clothes Campaign (CCC) in Europe and the Apparel Industry Partnership in the United States. The Business Roundtable, a business lobby group, documents more than 20 major multinationals in a range of industries that apply codes of conduct to their worldwide operations.[53] An increasing number of codes are subject to independent auditing.

Despite the growing incidence of such codes, publicity tends to focus much more on cases of abuse of labor rights. Where production is subcontracted, it may be difficult for principal firms to ensure that codes of conduct are observed. For example, while Nike formally employs about 20,000 people worldwide, there are an additional 500,000 people engaged in making Nike products (Figure 6.1). Corporate codes can be effective in improving conditions further down supply chains. In response to the Levi Strauss code, GrupM, a major employer in the free-trade zone of the Dominican Republic, undertook a number of improve-ments to conditions, including subsidized transport for workers, day-care centers, medical and dental care, and social-insurance benefits. These changes were instrumental in enabling the company to win contracts from other principals, including Liz Claiborne, Nike, and Gap.

Private codes of conduct have two principal shortcomings. First, their coverage is often limited. A number do not include even core labor standards. For instance, neither Wal-Mart nor Liz Claiborne includes in their codes the right of workers to join a union or engage in collective bargaining. Second, to achieve credibility, codes need to be subject to external monitoring. However, one study that examined monitoring of factories in China, Korea, and Indonesia by accounting giant PricewaterhouseCoopers suggested that a wide range of violations were overlooked.[54] Many companies, includ-ing Wal-Mart, Gap, and Disney, have preferred not to make their audits public. In recent months, a number of major businesses, including Nike and Reebok have published their audit reports on the website of the Fair Labor Association (FLA). While this is a step forward, there are still some shortcomings with the system, in that some basic rights are not considered, sites inspected are not named, and only 5 percent of factories have to be inspected. More positively, however, is the fact that the FLA audit does list what factories are doing to try to overcome identified problems.

SOCIAL LABELING

Social labeling takes a variety of forms. One is the use of NGO-registered trademarks such as RUGMARK. The RUGMARK

Figure 6.1   Nike is Vietnam's largest private employer, with 20,000 formally employed and another 500,000 engaged in making Nike products. This can make it difficult for such a far-flung company to ensure that codes of conduct are followed.

label guarantees that a rug bearing this mark has not been made by child labor (Figure 6.2). RUGMARK works with carpet makers in India, Nepal, and Pakistan and has certified six U.S. carpet importers.

A second variant is the international standard SA 8000, an auditable international standard for socially responsible trade. The standard, created by a group of NGOs and union and business representatives, is externally monitored and audited. The purpose is to allow socially responsible companies

Levi Strauss—Forming Multi-stakeholder Partnerships

Levi Strauss & Co., a privately owned U.S. company, is one the world's largest brand-name apparel manufacturers. The company owns brands including Levi's, Dockers, and Slates and employs 30,000 people worldwide. It has a head start on many human and labor rights issues given that it was the first multinational company in its sector to adopt a code. But perhaps most importantly, it has consistently used a multi-stakeholder approach to develop and implement its policy on working conditions.

In 1991, a cross-departmental project team began a two-year project that involved 25 internal and external stakeholder groups. It also conducted research on the conditions that workers experienced in the 600 to 700 subcontracting units that are based in 50 to 60 countries. The team considered the various needs and concerns of all parties. This process led to the formulation and adoption of guidelines, Levi Strauss's Terms of Engagement (ToE), in 1992. In-country managers became responsible for ensuring the implementation of these ToEs and were given specialist auditor training to do so.

Over the last seven years, Levi Strauss has been testing more intensive forms of multi-stakeholder engagement. This is part of the evolution of an internal monitoring process that has gone from a simple Q & A session to a detailed review about the dos and don'ts of implementing the key human rights elements. This has been an evolving process, the most recent step being a pilot project in the Dominican Republic (DR) that was designed to help answer the question of how to make internal monitoring more effective and therefore credible.

The problem is this. Professional auditors can be too expensive, can fail to understand the local situation well enough, can have insufficient access to workers to be able properly to verify the most important human rights issues, and can have limited credibility for the social verification task. Unions are perhaps the obvious "social partner" for this sort of work, but the business-union relationship is often very tense, with mutual recriminations and an adversarial history. Labor-friendly NGOs that have

to differentiate themselves from their competitors, particularly in industries with a questionable reputation. Well-known member companies include Avon, Dole, and Toys "R" Us.

Levi Strauss & Co., a privately owned U.S. company, is one of the world's largest brand-name apparel manufacturers.

the credibility to verify working conditions are often not well equipped for the task. And those NGOs that have the best capacity and credibility for this role often have the least developed relationship with contractors. Given this situation, Miriam Rodriguez, Levi Strauss's Latin America Regional Manager saw only one way forward: "We believed that if you could bring everyone to the table, we could achieve a better solution than any one party could do alone."

Source: *CSR (Corporate Social Responsibility) Business and Human Rights.*

Figure 6.2   RUGMARK is a global nonprofit organization working to end child labor and offer educational possibilities for children in India, Nepal, and Pakistan.

Third, some companies have invested in creating a socially responsible brand, the best known being the British-based Body Shop, which is closely identified with socially and environmentally responsible practices. It follows its own ethical code of conduct, publishes a large amount of verifiable information about its operations, and participates in community trade programs.

A fourth variant is social or ethical trading initiatives. The main market failure for labor standards is the lack of information consumers have regarding production processes and workplace conditions. Ethical trading initiatives such as Fair Trade, a label that guarantees that farmers and workers received a fair price for their product, seek to overcome this failure through the assurance that specified conditions are observed. The experience of a country such as Mexico, which made a rapid transition from being highly protectionist to a leading global free trader, is that globalization tends to favor large international businesses, not the many small-scale farmers, artisans, and small-business employees found within developing countries. These workers, cooperatives, and NGOs are now coming together to establish support networks that give them access to capital, technology, marketing know-how, and foreign distribution chains. While securing their livelihoods to some extent, fair trade markets also offer an alternative to current business practices, one that is founded more on equity and sustainable development. There are now a number of well-known fair trading networks including Fair Trade, TradeAid, The Max Havelaar Foundation, TransFair, Global Exchange, and Environmental Defense (Figure 6.3).

Fair trade networks incorporate a number of principles within their agreements, generally covering working conditions, control over various stages of value-adding, social and environmental responsibility, financial and management support, community benefit, and consumer education. The labor conditions usually stipulate a fair wage earned under healthy, safe conditions and transparency of business practices. The fair wage is achieved through higher prices possible because products target consumers willing to pay for the assurance of fair trade and working conditions.

To be effective, social labeling programs need to ensure certain conditions. First, they need to encompass all interested parties in an equitable partnership. This may mean businesses, labor unions, NGOs, and government bodies. Second, to achieve credibility, they need independent external monitoring to ensure adherence to the principles. Third, such programs need to incorporate effective enforcement mechanisms to ensure that violators can be identified, punished, and, if necessary, excluded.

Figure 6.3   The traditional organization of the coffee business allows individual growers to receive a very low return on their invested time and labor. In an effort to provide an alternative, Fair Trade Coffee was formed. Along with certifying coffee growers and sellers, TransFair, the non-profit organization that monitors the coffee market, guarantees farmers $1.29 per pound. The impact of the fair trade movement can be seen in the "Fair Trade Certified" label on these Millstone brand coffee beans, part of the Procter & Gamble product line. In July 2004, Procter & Gamble announced that it would expand sales of its more expensive coffees to benefit impoverished growers.

Social labeling and fair trade campaigns face a number of challenges. At the moment, they remain small and generally confined to niche market segments, such as specialty coffee, honey, and baseballs. In commodity industries, subsidies to foreign competitors and the instability of international commodity prices tend to undermine the "fair prices" assured to producers. Certification and fair trade labeling is expensive, and such costs may be difficult for producers to bear or to pass on to consumers of certain products. Public policy is generally indifferent towards fair trade, and consumer education and access to fair trade products both need to be improved.[55]

A further international proposal that, while of a more general nature, could be of value to labor, is to redesign the processes of globalization. In particular, the focus would shift from simply the efficiency benefits of globalization, which tend to be the preoccupation of business enterprises, to a greater consideration of the equity effects. In practice, this would mean greater sharing of the positive impacts of globalization coupled with attempts to minimize the negative effects. Labor could benefit from such restructuring both directly and indirectly. Directly, reform of globalization is likely to include wages and working conditions as well as labor's involvement in production processes. Indirectly, if reform increases growth rates in more developing countries, then, given the positive correlation between income and labor standards, labor could benefit. Such proposals are still at an early stage and how they might be implemented is as yet unclear.[56]

CONCLUSIONS

There is a general perception that globalization has been harmful to the interests of workers. This perception is encapsulated in the concept of "a race to the bottom." In labor market terms, globalization has been linked to the growth of the informal labor sector and declining wages for the least skilled. Rapid growth in international outsourcing is now threatening the employment and incomes of comparatively skilled workers in a range of service industries within developed countries.

These concerns have prompted a strident debate on the merits and most efficient forms of intervention. Over the past three decades, there has been a shift in perception away from policies that focus purely on the activities of multinational enterprises and those likely to distort international economic activity. The growth of global business—involving trade, investment, and offshore sourcing—has encouraged the search for more general and preferably market-based policies such as core labor standards, fair trade regimes, and social labeling. In many cases these initiatives need to be accompanied by complementary labor market policies that facilitate effective adjustment. We should also be aware that poor labor standards may be the result of weak local laws and enforcement and not solely the result of globalization.

Our discussion highlights a number of conclusions. First, some intervention can be beneficial in terms of both efficiency and equity. For example, core labor standards that eliminate forced labor, discrimination, or the employment of children are likely to improve welfare. On the other hand, mandating economic labor standards on minimum wages or overtime rates at an international level is likely to be counterproductive. While it is possible that core labor standards may be incorporated into future trade agreements, particularly regional or bilateral agreements, it is unlikely that economic standards will be included within multilateral trade and investment agreements.

Second, how these standards should be implemented and enforced is also debatable. Historically, this responsibility has been embodied within the International Labor Organization (ILO), but critics have expressed concern regarding the ability of the ILO to enforce such standards. More recent proposals argue for closer links between the ILO and WTO.

Third, approaches that utilize market forces to improve the welfare of labor are finding increasing favor. Corporate codes of conduct, social labeling, and ethical trading programs provide opportunities for informed consumers to exercise a preference for socially responsible products and the proliferation of high standards. Coupled with improved consumer information and education, such approaches can help encourage a "race to the top" without restricting trade and growth.

Fourth, the separation of policies designed to deal with the difficulties stemming from trade, foreign investment, and outsourcing is unhelpful. The reality in the global marketplace is that decisions in these areas are increasingly unified under the control of MNEs. If managers make such decisions in an integrated way, fragmented and distinct policies are likely to increase market distortions to the detriment of efficient resource use.

Fifth, in a number of cases policy choices should be seen as complementary. Where workers in developing countries benefit from the introduction of higher labor standards and remain competitive, developed country governments should be focusing on education, training, and innovation policies in an attempt to lift more of their work force out of a situation of direct competition. The small scale of ethical trading programs means that for the foreseeable future they may complement, but are unlikely to replace, the pursuit of core labor standards. There may also be a conflict between the introduction of labor standards and the desirability of maintaining flexible labor markets. Overly restrictive regulations, particularly economic standards, could impede the efficient adjustment of labor markets.

Finally, in the long term economic growth provides the key driver of improved standards. In this case, every encouragement should be given to freer trade, investment, and technology flows. Disruption and labor market adjustment resulting from increased growth in developing countries need to be addressed through complementary education, training, and flexible labor market operations.

Conclusions

In this chapter we will review the effects of globalization on labor and highlight the most significant conclusions. After reading this book, you should understand that the topic of globalization and labor is important, controversial, and, in many ways, poorly understood. Its importance is apparent: The global era is redefining many aspects of life, including labor market participation. For those with the requisite skills, appropriate experience, and ambition, the working world has never been as exciting or enriching as it is today. Boundless opportunities exist to live and work in almost any part of the world and to experience new cultures, ideas, and ways of doing things. On the other hand, individuals lacking the skills and experience that are valued in the world economy face the possibility of increased insecurity and instability and declining real income. Inequality of opportunity and reward is a characteristic of the global era. Globalization brings benefits and costs, and opportunities and threats. The challenge for policy makers is to capture and fairly distribute the undoubted benefits, while minimizing the costs. While this is a demanding task, it is a worthwhile undertaking, since globalization represents the most powerful engine of economic development at work in the world today.

Globalization is controversial for two main reasons. First, its impact is uneven. It creates winners and losers. Critics argue that too much of the gains are captured by the wealthy countries and the multinational enterprises based in those countries. While it is generally accepted that those benefiting from globalization outnumber those who are disadvantaged, a straightforward comparison of these two groups is not possible. To believe that one can compare how much an affluent consumer benefits from lower import prices to the dramatic loss of livelihood and self-worth experienced by a worker laid off because of import competition is to trivialize the impact of globalization. Second, there is considerable debate regarding the magnitude and value of both the benefits and costs of globalization. Critics argue that the benefits of globalization are far less worthwhile than economists assume. They question the distribution of benefits and whether the world environment can sustain the high rates of economic growth and development that globalization promises. Critics also suggest that the costs are not just economic and that globalization embodies the transfer of ideologies and cultural values threatening traditional societies.

The impact of globalization on labor is also poorly understood. There are a number of places in this book where we have presented qualified arguments or have had to accept that we simply do not know how distinctive and significant a role globalization plays. This is particularly the case when we examine employment and wage change. Further research, using better conceptual and measurement tools, is urgently needed.

In spite of all these uncertainties and controversies, we can, however, draw some important conclusions.

THE REALITY OF GLOBALIZATION

The first and perhaps firmest conclusion is that globalization is now a reality for much of the world economy and a sizable group of workers. Few economies can escape the competitive pressures that result from trade, foreign investment, and technology transfer. More recently we have seen a dramatic growth in offshoring of work that shows few signs of abating.[57] These developments have been facilitated by continuing technological development and falling costs of transport, communication, and control. While only a minority of workers are directly impacted by these processes, indirect effects are sizable and likely to increase in the future.

We have already highlighted the fact that globalization brings both benefits and costs. It has certainly contributed to higher rates of economic growth in a number of developing countries and has lifted significant numbers of people out of poverty.[58] For a country such as the United States, world economic and political leadership has meant increasing engagement with the forces of globalization. Imports as a share of U.S. gross domestic product (GDP) rose from 5 percent to 13.1 percent between 1965 and 1999. Similarly, exports in GDP doubled to more than 10 percent over the same period. Accommodating the forces of globalization is a reality for increasing numbers of workers. It is also important to note that there is a disturbing negative side to globalization. As business has prospered under globalization, so has crime. The international drug, human trafficking, and sex trades bring misery to the lives of many millions around the world.

THE DYNAMICS OF GLOBALIZATION

A second conclusion is that despite critics and setbacks, globalization is likely to continue to be a powerful and potent force in the world economy.[59] We should avoid believing that somehow there is a fixed level of output and jobs in the world and that globalization's primary impact is in moving these around. This is totally wrong; we are still a long way from economic limits to output and employment growth and we are not powerless to influence the global distribution of these.

For example, while we hear much talk about leading multinational enterprises transferring jobs from developed to developing countries, the reality is far more complex. Companies such

Will Offshoring Affect Europe in the Same Way as It Has the United States?

Forrester Research, a major U.S. consultancy, has recently looked at the question of whether offshoring will affect Europe to the extent as it has the U.S. They surveyed 247 user companies and 19 international offshore service providers to try to gauge future intentions. European firms face the same pressures as U.S. businesses to move work offshore. In all the developed countries, offshoring provides access to lower cost labor and is driven by fierce competition.

Forrester concludes that Europe will lose a cumulative 1.2 million jobs to offshore locations by 2015. This is less than half the forecast 3.3 million jobs they see the United States shedding over the same period. The United Kingdom and Ireland are the European leaders in offshoring. The most aggressive users of offshore locations are financial firms, and the job shifts will be greatest for computing and clerical workers.

The research highlights two important points. First, protectionist barriers such as bans on offshoring or controls on redundancy may slow, but are unlikely to stem, the shift of jobs. Competitive pressure is simply too strong and employers will find ways around such impediments. Second, the competitive advantages of lower labor costs and greater flexibility offered by offshoring mean that countries that resist the process are likely to experience competitive disadvantage. This will be a particular concern for countries such as Germany, France, Italy, and the Netherlands, which have been the slowest to use offshoring.

Source: A. Parker, "Two-Speed Europe: Why 1 Million Jobs Will Move Offshore." *Forrester Research* (August 2004).

as IBM and Intel certainly are creating jobs in China and India, but the reality is that they are adding just as many if not more, and generally more highly skilled, positions in the United States. Where we see firms shedding jobs or closing down, this can usually be traced to recessions, fierce competition, or technological change. Of course, these factors are related to globalization, but the view that jobs are simply being transferred to low-cost countries is naïve. While the most recent U.S. recession saw very slow employment recovery, better quality jobs are now starting to appear.

The processes of globalization are unlikely to be reversed or abandoned. There is simply too much at stake. Continued affluence in the United States and Western Europe, recovery in Japan, and rising welfare in China, India, Latin America, and Eastern Europe all depend on the power of globalization. Any hope of helping the world's very poorest in Africa, the Middle East, and South Asia is also likely to be driven by global economic growth, which has proved far more powerful than the alternatives such as foreign aid. More plausible is a modification of globalization through policy interventions that seek to ameliorate the costs of globalization and to ensure that the benefits are shared more widely. This might also go some way to placate the anti-globalist protestors who have been so vocal in recent years. Recent discussions of the problem of poverty have focused much more on the need to raise productivity, which is one of the most significant effects of globalization.[60]

GLOBALIZATION AND TECHNOLOGY

The relationship between globalization and technology is complex. As we have seen, wage and employment changes that cannot be explained by globalization are generally attributed to technological change. However, this is not a valid representation of reality. Most forms of global economic activity—trade, foreign investment, and offshore sourcing—all embody significant technology. Indeed, multinational enterprises, companies at the very forefront of economic globalization, are also the most significant vehicles for the development and diffusion of new technologies. The links between global economic activities and technology mean that globalization plays a greater role in determining labor market outcomes than has been previously acknowledged.

GLOBALIZATION AND THE MANAGEMENT CHALLENGE

We have also seen that globalization has had a sizable impact on labor organization and management approaches to the labor resource. The competitive pressures resulting from globalization have reinforced the need for economic approaches to the management of human resources, highlighting the need for cooperation, stability, and flexibility. The decline of union influence has weakened the support traditionally available to the most vulnerable workers in the workplace. In a number of industries, companies have utilized new work forms including part-time, casual forms of employment that have contributed to the growth of informal labor markets and declining levels of union representation. To maintain a significant position in the foreseeable future, organized labor will have to rethink traditional approaches to their role in the workplace and their ability to recruit non-traditional work groups such as older workers. At the same time there is strong demand for highly skilled global managers who are able to organize and manage operations worldwide.

GLOBALIZATION, LABOR ISSUES, AND POLICY INTERVENTION

The widespread recognition of the adjustment costs generated by globalization has brought considerable interest in the design of appropriate policy interventions. As we have seen, a variety of proposals have been aired and a number of trends are readily discernible in policy thinking. Policies that minimize labor market distortions, that facilitate free trade, and that do not focus unduly on the relative bargaining power of labor and business enjoy increasing acceptance. However, such market-based policies are still not well understood.

A further problem is policy fragmentation. Policy fragmentation—separate policies that focus on trade, foreign direct investment, or offshoring—does not reflect the increasingly integrative nature of decision making on these issues within global corporations. We might expect to see more attention paid to understanding the integrative and interactive nature of these issues in future policy development. It is also worth noting that newer policy choices such as voluntary codes of conduct and ethical trading programs provide an alternative to traditional regimes. Policy diversity between countries with different levels of income is to be expected. While developing countries seek to improve their core labor standards, developed countries need to maintain and facilitate labor market flexibility, education, and training.

To maximize the benefits of globalization, countries also need to acknowledge the importance of domestic policy responses. In this sense, countries that feel powerless in the face of globalization can mediate its immediate impact through effective policy choice and preparation. Investments in appropriate infrastructure and institutions can influence the likely impact of global forces and opportunities to maximize the positive effects of globalization. In theory, globalization should not contribute to the growth of inequality within developing countries (since the demand for low-cost labor increases), except through increasing the vulnerability of a country to external shocks, such as exchange rate changes, that can result from greater openness. However, it is useful to distinguish between short- and long-term adjustments. Opening an economy to freer trade may worsen income inequality in the short term; the longer-term effects depend in part on the domestic policy response and existing income levels.[61]

FURTHER RESEARCH

Finally, it should be apparent that there are a number of areas relating to globalization and labor where we cannot currently draw firm conclusions. Further and more sophisticated research is required on these topics. Considerable uncertainty exists regarding the effects of globalization on employment levels, income distribution, and working conditions. More generally, globalization appears to be changing labor market dynamics, including economic recovery and social mobility, in complex ways. Recent work is beginning to address some of these issues and suggests the value of more sophisticated modelling[62] as well as recognition that the gross costs of labor market adjustment far exceed those normally considered.[63] This research confirms two important considerations. The first is the need to tie further economic openness to the provision of supportive adjustment policies. This now seems to be a necessary condition for obtaining public support for continuing economic openness.[64] The second consideration is the difficulty of designing optimal policies where the adjustment processes within firms vary. The bluntness of current policies means that they are unlikely to target adjustment problems effectively. Our discussion highlights the need for more and better work on a topic that is likely to be of major public concern for the foreseeable future.

Comparative advantage—The advantage possessed by a country engaged in international trade if it can produce a given good at lower resource output cost than other countries.

Competitive advantage—A unique blend of activities, assets, relationships, history, and market conditions that an organization exploits in order to differentiate itself from its competitors and thus create value.

Elasticity of demand for labor—The percentage change in employment caused by a 1 percent change in the wage rate.

Expatriate—A person who leaves her or his native country to live and work in another.

Export processing zones (EPZs)—Industrial areas designated by a government to provide tax and other incentives to export firms.

Foreign direct investment (FDI)—Investment by a firm based in one country in actual productive capacity or other real assets in another country.

Globalization—The trend towards a single, integrated and inter-dependent world; also, the breaking down of traditional barriers between countries allowing the movement of goods, capital, people, and information.

Gross domestic product (GDP)—The total market value of goods and services produced domestically during a given period.

Host-country nationals (HCNs)—Employees who are nationals of the country hosting the affiliate operations of a multinational enterprise (MNE).

Human resources management (HRM)—The set of activities directed at attracting, developing, and maintaining the effective work force necessary to achieve a firm's objectives

Import penetration—The percentage ratio of imports to home demand, where home demand is defined as total producers' sales plus imports minus exports.

Inpatriation—The transfer of international managers from their overseas assignments to the home-country market on a permanent or semipermanent basis.

International Labor Organization (ILO)—The United Nations agency concerned with the interests of labor.

Jobless growth—Output growth without commensurate increases in employment.

Labor market churn—The continuous change in labor markets that result from economic forces.

Liberalization—The act of removing economic restrictions.

***Maquiladora* plant**—A production facility, along the U.S./Mexico border, that processes or assembles components into finished products.

Multinational enterprise (MNE)—An enterprise that owns or controls value-adding activities in more than one country.

National income—The sum of the incomes of all individuals in the economy earned in the form of wages, interest, rents, and profits. It includes transfer payments and is calculated before any deductions are taken for income taxes.

Non-governmental organization (NGO)—An association based on the common interests of members, individuals, or institutions that has no governmental status or function, is not created by a government, and does not have an agenda set or implemented by a government.

Offshoring or offshore sourcing—The transfer overseas of manufacturing, information technology, and back-office services to take advantage of lower-cost labor.

Organization for Economic Cooperation and Development (OECD)—A grouping of industrialized countries formed to promote the economic well being of its members and to contribute to worldwide development.

Parent-country nationals (PCNs)—Employees who are nationals of the MNE parent country.

Protectionism—The process of government economic protection for domestic producers through restrictions on foreign competition.

Sweatshop—A factory characterized by intense production where workers are typically paid by piecework and restricted from forming unions.

Tariff—A tax levied on imported products.

Third-country nationals (TCNs)—Employees who are nationals of a country other than that of the parent firm or overseas affiliates.

World Trade Organization (WTO)—An institution, which grew out of the General Agreement on Tariffs and Trade (GATT), that oversees international trade issues, resolves trade disputes, and enforces the GATT trade pact.

1 M. J. Slaughter and K. F. Shreve, *Globalization and the Perceptions of American Workers*. Washington, D.C.: Institute for International Economics, 2001.

2 A. Maddison, *Monitoring the World Economy*. Paris: OECD Publications, 1995.

3 UNCTAD, *World Investment Report 1993: Transnational Corporations and Integrated International Production*. Geneva and New York: United Nations Conference on Trade and Development, 1993.

4 S. Anderson and J. Cavanagh, *Top 200: The Rise of Corporate Global Power*. Washington, D.C.: Institute of Policy Studies, 2000.

5 UNCTAD, *World Investment Report 2000: Cross-Border Mergers and Acquisitions and Development*. Geneva and New York: United Nations Conference on Trade and Development, 2000.

6 Ibid.

7 J. C. Cooper, *Business Week* (Jan. 26, 2004): 33.

8 M. J. Slaughter, "Production Transfer Within Multinational Enterprises and American Wages." *Journal of International Economics* vol. 50 (2000): 449–472.

9 P. Legrain, *Open World: The Truth About Globalisation*. London, Abacus: 2004.

10 E. Appelbaum, A. Bernhardt, and R.J. Mumane (eds.), *Low-Wage America: How Employers are Reshaping Opportunity in the Workplace*. New York: Russell Sage Foundation, 2003.

11 "Mexico: Was NAFTA Worth It?" *Business Week* (Dec. 22, 2003): 34–41.

12 International Labor Organization, *Labour Practices in the Footwear, Leather, Textiles and Clothing Industries*. Geneva: ILO, 2000.

13 C. V. Prestowitz, "Can We Survive Technology Transfer?" In *Software and Hardhats: Technology and Workers in the 21st Century*. Washington, D.C.: Labor Policy Institute, 1992, pp. 61–70.

14 M. Lind, *The Next American Nation: The New Nationalism and the Fourth American Revolution*. New York: Free Press 1995. 203

15 V. Agrawal and D. Farrell, "Who Wins in Offshoring?" *The McKinsey Quarterly* no. 4 (2003).

16 "The New Geography of the IT Industry." *The Economist* (July 19, 2003): 47–49.

17 A. Tonelson, *The Race to the Bottom: Why a Worldwide Worker Surplus and Uncontrolled Free Trade are Sinking American Living Standards*. Boulder, CO: Westview Press, 2002.

18 R. Kaplinsky, "Export Processing Zones in the Dominican Republic: Transforming Manufactures into Commodities." *World Development* vol. 22, no.3 (1993): 1851–1865; H. Schmitz, "Small Shoemakers and Fordist Giants: Tales of a Supercluster." *World Development* vol. 23, no. 1 (1995): 9–28.

19 J. Rifkin, *The End of Work: The Decline of the Global Labor Force and the Dawn of the Post-Market Era*. New York: J.P. Tarcher, 1996.

20 M. Carr and M .A. Chen, "Globalization and the Informal Economy: How Global Trade and Investment Impact on the Working Poor." ILO Employment Sector Working Paper on the Informal Economy. Geneva: ILO, 2002.

21 T. Larsson, *The Race to the Top: The Real Story of Globalization*. Washington, DC: Cato Institute, 2001.

22 J. Norberg, *In Defense of Global Capitalism*. Washington, D.C.: Cato Institute, 2003.

23 ILO, *Investing in Every Child, An Economic Study of the Costs and Benefits of Eliminating Child Labour.* Geneva: International Labor Organization, 2004.

24 Legrain, *Open World.*

25 L. G. Kletzer, *Job Loss From Imports: Measuring the Costs.* Washington, D.C.: Institute for International Economics, 2001.

26 J. D. Sachs A.M. Warner, "Economic Reform and the Process of Global Integration." *Brookings Papers on Economic Activity* Vol.1 (1995): 1–95.

27 See, for example, M. Lundberg and L. Squire, "The Simultaneous Evolution of Growth and Inequality" (1999) and D. Dollar and A. Kraay, "Growth is Good for the Poor" (2001), both World Bank Research Papers.

28 G. Firebaugh, *The New Geography of Global Income Inequality.* Cambridge: Harvard University Press, 2003.

29 Earnings deflated for changes in the price level (inflation).

30 P. Gottschalk, "Changes in Inequality of Family Income in Seven Industrialized Countries." *American Economic Review* Vol. 83, No. 2 (May 1993): 136–142.

31 Oxfam, *Rigged Rules and Double Standards: Trade, Globalisation and the Fight Against Poverty.* Oxford, UK: Oxfam, 2002.

32 R. C. Feenstra and G. H. Hanson, "Foreign Direct Investment and Relative Wages: Evidence from Mexico's Maquiladoras." *Journal of International Economics* Vol. 42 (1997): 371–393.

33 W. P. Cline, *Trade and Income Distribution.* Washington, D.C.: Institute for International Economics, 1997.

34 R.B. Freeman and L.F. Katz, "Rising Wage Inequality: The United States Versus Other Advanced Countries." In R.B. Freeman, ed. *Working Under Different Rules.* New York: Russell Sage Foundation, 1994.

35 UNCTAD, *World Investment Report 2002: Transnational Corporations and Export Competitiveness.* New York and Geneva: United Nations, 2002.

36 The union wage premium refers to the extent to which a union member's wage exceeds that of an otherwise comparable non-unionized worker.

37 R. E. Baldwin, *The Decline of U.S. Labor Unions and the Role of Trade.* Washington, DC: Institute for International Economics, 2003.

38 H. Farber and A. Krueger, *Union Membership in the United States: The Decline Continues.* National Bureau of Economic Research Working Paper 4216 (1992).

39 Baldwin, *The Decline of U.S. Labor Unions.*

40 ILO, *Labour Practices in the Footwear, Leather, Textiles and Clothing Industries.* Geneva: ILO, 2000.

41 P. Enderwick, *Multinational Business and Labour.* Beckenham: Croom Helm, 1985.

42 K. Bronfenbrenner, "Plant Closings, Plant-Closing Threats, Union Organizing and the NAFTA." *Multinational Monitor* Vol. 18, No. 3 (March 1997).

43 H. Lewis III and J.D. Richardson, *Why Global Commitment Really Matters!* Washington, D.C.: Institute for International Economics, 2001.

44 S. Black et al., *Globalizing People Through International Assignments.* Reading, MA: Addison-Wesley, 1999.

45 V. Pucik and T. Saba, "Selecting and Developing the Global Versus the Expatriate Manager: A Review of the State-of-the-Art" *Human Resource Planning* Vol. 21, No. 4 (1998): 40–54.

46 J. S. Black, A. J. Morrison, and H.B. Gregersen, *Global Explorers: The Next Generation of Leaders.* New York: Routledge, 1999.

47 N. J. Adler and D.N. Izraeli, *Competitive Frontiers: Women Managers in a Global Economy.* Cambridge, MA: Blackwell, 1994.

48 The OECD identifies five core labor standards: (1) prohibition of forced labor; (2) freedom of association; (3) the right to organize and bargain collectively; (4) elimination of the exploitation of child labor; and (5) non-discrimination in employment.

49 Organization for Economic Cooperation and Development. *Trade, Employment and Labour Standards. A Study of Core Workers Rights and International Trade.* Paris: OECD, 1996.

50 D. H. Rosen, *Behind the Open Door: Foreign Enterprises in the Chinese Marketplace.* Washington, D.C.: Institute for International Economics, 1999.

51 K. E. Maskus, *Should Core Labor Standards be Imposed Through International Trade Policy?* Washington, D.C.: World Bank, International Trade Division, 1997.

52 L. Kletzer, *Job Loss From Imports: Measuring the Costs.* Washington, D.C.: Institute for International Economics, 2001.

53 Business Roundtable, *Corporate Social Responsibility in China: Practices by U.S. Companies.* Washington, D.C.: The Business Roundtable, 2000.

54 D. O'Rourke, *Monitoring the Monitors: A Critique of Price Waterhouse Cooper's Labor Monitoring.* Boston: Massachusetts Institute of Technology, 2000.

55 If you are interested in fair trade and related issues the following are useful resources: Fair Trade Federation (http://www.fairtradefederation.com), an organization that promotes partnerships between marketers in North America and producers in Asia, Africa, Latin America, and other parts of the world; Fair Trade Resource Network (http://www.fairtraderesource .org/about/html) raises consumer awareness about fair trade by conducting research, providing information, and facilitating fair trade networking and organizing; Global Exchange (http://www.globalexchange .org) supports fair trade through advocacy and marketing, and its website includes a large number of resources related to fair trade;TransFair USA (http://www.transfairusa.org) is a nonprofit certification organization for fair trade products in America that works to increase the availability of fair trade certified products and to increase consumer awareness; Fairtrade Labeling Organizations International (http://www.fairtrade.net) is an international umbrella organization of fair trading labeling initiatives.

56 See, for example, J. H. Dunning (ed.), *Making Globalization Good: The Moral Challenges of Global Capitalism.* Oxford: Oxford University Press, 2003.

57 Indeed, in recognition of its importance, the consulting firm A. T. Kearney has recently published an index ranking the attractiveness of countries as locations for offshoring.

58 However, because some of these countries, such as India and China, are very large in population terms, the number of people who have benefited is much larger.

59 Recent events that had a negative impact on globalization include the Asian Financial Crisis of 1997, the terrorist attacks of September 11, 2001, and the limited progress of the Doha trade rounds.

60 See, for example, W. Lewis, *The Power of Productivity: Wealth, Poverty, and the Threat to Global Stability.* Chicago: University of Chicago, 2004.

61 B. Milanovic, "Can We Discern The Effect of Globalization on Income Distribution?" *World Bank Policy Research Working Paper 2876.* Washington D.C.: World Bank, 2002.

62 C. Davidson and S. J. Matusz, *International Trade and Labor Markets: Theory, Evidence and Policy*

Implications. Kalamazoo, MI: W.E. Upjohn Institute for Employment Research, 2004.

63 M. W. Klein, S. Schuh, and R. K. Triest, *Job Creation, Job Destruction and International Competition.* Kalamazoo, MI: W. E. Upjohn Institute for Employment Research, 2003.

64 K. F. Scheve and M. J. Slaughter, *Globalization and the Perceptions of American Workers.* Washington, D.C.: Institute for International Economics, 2001.

Adler, N. J., and D. N. Izraeli. *Competitive Frontiers: Women Managers in a Global Economy*. Cambridge, MA: Blackwell, 1994.

Agrawal, V., and D. Farrell. Who Wins in Offshoring? *The McKinsey Quarterly* No. 4 (2003).

Appelbaum, E., A. Bernhardt, and R. J. Mumane (eds.). *Low-Wage America: How Employers are Reshaping Opportunity in the Workplace*. New York: Russell Sage Foundation, 2003.

Bardham, A. D., and C. Kroll. *The New Wave of Outsourcing*. University of California at Berkeley: Fisher Centre for Real Estate and Urban Economics Research Report, 2003.

Black, J. S., A. J. Morrison, and H. B. Gregersen. *Global Explorers: The Next Generation of Leaders*. New York: Routledge, 1999.

Black, S., H. Gregersen, M. Mendenhall, and L. Stroh. *Globalizing People Through International Assignments*. Reading, MA: Addison-Wesley, 1999.

Bonache, J., C. Brewster, and V. Suutari. "Expatriation: A Developing Research Agenda." *Thunderbird International Business Review* Vol. 43, No. 1 (2001): 3-20.

Bronfenbrenner, K. "Plant Closings, Plant-Closing Threats, Union Organizing and the NAFTA." *Multinational Monitor* Vol. 18, No. 3 (March 1997).

Carr, M., and M. A. Chen. *Globalization and the Informal Economy: How Global Trade and Investment Impact on the Working Poor*. Geneva: ILO Employment Sector Working Paper on the Informal Economy, 2002

Cline, W. P. *Trade and Income Distribution*. Washington, D.C.: Institute for International Economics, 1997.

Dowling, P. J., R. S. Schuler, and D. Welch. *International Dimensions of Human Resource Management*, 2nd edition. Belmont, CA: Wadsworth, 1994.

Cooke, W. M. (ed.) *Multinational Companies and Transnational Workplace Issues.* New York: Greenwood Publishing, 2002.

De Vries, M. F. R., and Florent-Treacy, E. "Global Leadership from A to Z: Creating High Commitment Organizations." *Organizational Dynamics* Vol. 30, No. 4 (2002): 295–309.

Drezner, D. "The Outsourcing Bogeyman." *Foreign Affairs* (May/June 2004).

Economist. "A Survey of Outsourcing." *The Economist* (Nov. 13–19, 2004).

Enderwick, P. *Multinational Business and Labour.* Beckenham: Croom Helm, 1985.

Engardio, P., A. Bernstein, and M. Kripalani. "The New Global Job Shift." *Business Week* (February 3, 2003).

Feenstra, R. C., and G. H. Hanson. "Foreign Direct Investment and Relative Wages: Evidence from Mexico's Maquiladoras." *Journal of International Economics* Vol. 42 (1997): 371–393.

Firebaugh, G. *The New Geography of Global Income Inequality.* Boston: Harvard University Press, 2003.

Freeman, R. B., and L. F. Katz. "Rising Wage Inequality: The United States versus Other Advanced Countries." In R.B. Freeman (ed.), *Working Under Different R*ules. New York: Russell Sage Foundation, 1994.

Harris, H. "Women in International Management: Why Are They Not Selected?" In C. Brewster and H. Harris (eds.). *International HRM: Contemporary Issues in Europe.* London: Routledge, 1994.

Harvey, M., C. Speier, and M. M. Novicevic. "The Role of Inpatriation in Global Staffing." *International Journal of Human Resource Management* Vol. 10, No. 3 (1999): 457–475.

ILO. *Labour Practices in the Footwear, Leather, Textiles and Clothing Industries.* Geneva: ILO, 2000.

Kletzer, L.G. *Job Loss From Imports: Measuring the Costs.* Washington, D.C.: Institute for International Economics, 2001.

Larsson, T. *The Race to the Top: The Real Story of Globalization.* Washington, D.C.: Cato Institute 2001.

Legrain, P. *Open World: The Truth About Globalisation.* London: Abacus, 2002.

Mann, C. *Globalisation of IT Services and White Collar Jobs: The Next Wave of Productivity Growth.* Washington, D.C.: Institute for International Economics, 2003.

Maskus, K. E. *Should Core Labor Standards be Imposed Through International Trade Policy?* Washington, D.C.: World Bank, International Trade Division, 1997.

McCarthy, J. "3.3m US Services Jobs To Go Offshore." Forrester Research (November 2002).

McKinsey Global Institute. *Offshoring: Is It a Win-Win Game?* San Francisco: MGI, 2003.

Micklethwait, J., and A. Woolridge. *A Future Perfect: The Challenge and Hidden Promise of Globalization.* London: Heinemann, 2003.

Norberg, J. *In Defense of Global Capitalism.* Washington, D.C.: Cato Institute, 2003.

Organization for Economic Cooperation and Development. *Trade, Employment and Labour Standards: A Study of Core Workers Rights and International Trade.* Paris: OECD, 1996.

Oxfam. *Rigged Rules and Double Standards: Trade, Globalisation and the Fight Against Poverty.* Oxford, UK: Oxfam, 2002.

Parker, A. "Two Speed Europe: Why 1 Million Jobs Will Move Offshore." Forrester Research (August 2004).

Pucik, V. Globalization and Human Resource Management. In V. Pucik, N. Tichy, and C. K. Barnett (eds.) *Globalizing Management.* New York: Wiley, 1992.

Pucik, V., and T. Saba. "Selecting and Developing the Global Versus the Expatriate Manager: A Review of the State-of-the-Art." *Human Resource Planning* Vol. 21, No. 4 (1998): 40–54.

Rodrik, D. *Has Globalization Gone Too Far?* Washington, D.C.: Institute for International Economics, 1998.

Rosenzweig, P. M., and Nohria, N. "Influences on Human Resource Management in Multinational Corporations." *Journal of International Business Studies* Vol. 20, No. 2 (1994): 229–251.

Sachs, J. D., and A. M. Warner. "Economic Reform and the Process of Global Integration." *Brookings Papers on Economic Activity* Vol. 1 (1995): 1–95.

Slaughter, M. J., and K. F. Shreve. *Globalization and the Perceptions of American Workers.* Washington, D.C.: Institute for International Economics, 2001.

Slaughter, M. J. "Production Transfer Within Multinational Enterprises and American Wages." *Journal of International Economics* Vol. 50 (2000): 449–472.

Tonelson, A. *The Race to the Bottom: Why a Worldwide Worker Surplus and Uncontrolled Free Trade are Sinking American Living Standards.* Boulder, CO: Westview Press, 2002.

Peter Enderwick is a Professor of International Business at Aukland University of Technology, Aukland, New Zealand. He is also an Adjunct Professor at the University of South Australia, Adelaide and Visiting Professor at Thammasat Business School, Thammasat University, Bangkok, Thailand. He has published a number of books and papers on international business and labor, has undertaken consultancy work for the United Nations in this area, and has taught in several European and Asian countries.

James Bacchus is Chairman of the Global Trade Practice Group of the international law firm Greenberg Traurig, Professional Association. He is also a visiting professor of international law at Vanderbilt University Law School. He served previously as a special assistant to the United States Trade Representative; as a Member of the Congress of the United States, from Florida; and as a Member, for eight years, and Chairman, for two terms, of the Appellate Body of the World Trade Organization. His book, *Trade and Freedom*, was published by Cameron May in London in 2004, and is now in its third edition worldwide.

Ilan Alon, Ph.D., is Associate Professor of International Business at the Crummer Graduate School of Business of Rollins College. He holds a Ph.D in International Business and Economics from Kent State University. He currently teaches courses on Business in the Global Environment and Emerging Markets: China in the business curriculum as well as International Trade and Economics in the economics curriculum.